105 Places You Must Visit in Los Angeles

From Hidden Gems to Iconic Landmarks, Discover the Incredible City of Angels!

Anne Parke

ISBN: 978-1-962496-08-7

For questions, please reach out to Support@OakHarborPress.com

Please consider leaving a review!

Just visit: OakHarborPress.com/Reviews

FREE BONUS

SCAN ME!

GET OUR NEXT BOOK FOR FREE!
Scan or go to:
OakHarborPress.com/Free

Table of Contents:

How to Use This Book

Welcome to your very own adventure guide to exploring the many wonders of the city of Los Angeles. Not only does this book offer the most wonderful places to visit and sights to see in the vibrant city, but it provides GPS coordinates for Google Maps to make exploring that much easier.

Adventure Guide

Sorted by region, this guide offers over 100 amazing wonders found in Los Angeles for you to see and explore. They can be visited in any order, and this book will help you keep track of where you've been and where to look forward to going next. Each section describes the area or place, what to look for, the physical address, and what you may need to bring along.

GPS Coordinates

As you can imagine, not all of the locations in this book have a physical address. Fortunately, some of our listed wonders are either located within a National Park or Reserve or near another landmark. For those that are not associated with a specific location, it is easiest to map it using GPS coordinates.

Luckily, Google has a system of codes that converts the coordinates into pin-drop locations that Google Maps can interpret and navigate.

Each adventure in this guide includes GPS coordinates along with a physical address whenever it is available.

It is important that you are prepared for poor cell signals. It is recommended that you route your location and ensure that the directions are accessible offline. Depending on your device and the distance of some locations, you may need to travel with a backup battery source.

Los Angeles's History

The Chumash and Tongva Native American tribes once resided in modern-day Los Angeles. The town was named *El Pueblo de Nuestra Señora la Reina de los Ángeles*, which translates to "The Town of Our Lady the Queen of the Angels of Porcincula." A group of 44 people from 14 families representing Native American, African, and European heritage traveled more than 1,000 miles across the desert in 1781 to claim the land. Over time, this neighborhood would expand under the flags of Spain and Mexico. Eventually, the town became the city of Los Angeles, one of the largest metropolitan areas in the world.

Los Angeles takes great pride in its history, as seen on its flag and city seal. Neighborhoods are celebrated for maintaining their origins through special events, museums, food, and more. Today, Los Angeles is a melting pot of culture, with over 121 neighborhoods partially or fully contained within Los Angeles County.

When most people think of Los Angeles, they think of palm trees and the sun, not to mention the city's link to the film industry, which makes it a popular destination for travelers. From the iconic Hollywood sign to picturesque walking trails and world-famous concert halls to fantastic adventure parks, Los Angeles has something for everyone.

Food and Culture

With a history steeped in culture, it's no wonder that Los Angeles has a fantastic food selection. From classy steakhouses to some of the best noodles in the world, a vacation can easily be based on food alone.

Avocado is one of California's most prized foods. Whether enjoying guacamole or avocado ice cream, this power food is at its peak in Los Angeles. When visiting, check out Dinette in Echo Park, where diners can enjoy a slice of thick Texas toast with avocado, chili flakes, parsley, and salt—the heartiest avocado toast around.

Seafood is another staple in Los Angeles, including dishes like cioppino. Seafood can be found at great restaurants like Cameron's Seafood & Market or the Water Grill. Seafood of the highest quality served in various delectable ways is available in every nook of the city, from pricey upscale raw bars to neighborhood you-buy-we-fry outlets. The diversity and quantity of Los Angeles's seafood scene make it a "must try" while vacationing.

Originating in Los Angeles, the French Dip sandwich is a classic that many know and love, so it's a great option for visitors to try while in town. The basics of the French Dip are simple: thinly sliced roast beef is heaped into a French roll coated in beef au jus. For a taste of history straight from the source, go to Philippe's on the edges of Chinatown in Los Angeles. According to legend, Philippe Mathieu, a French immigrant who founded Philippe's, accidentally created the sandwich in 1918. What was originally an error has become a Los Angeles institution. Just like Philippe's sandwich, the eatery is straightforward and reliable. Food is served on basic paper plates, and customers place their orders at a long counter. Don't forget to use some of Philippe's hot mustard, offered on every table and almost as well-known as the dip.

Guests in the mood for Chinese should head to the San Gabriel Valley. The San Gabriel Valley is well known around the country for having several excellent, authentic Chinese eateries. To experience the best *xiaolongbao*, or soup dumplings, guests should visit the Shanghai Dumpling House. The delicious dumplings from Shanghai Dumpling House have some of the thinnest skins in the industry and should be handled with extreme care.

Bars & Nightclubs

Los Angeles has upped its nightlife scene in recent years with everything from dance clubs to bars. With a well-connected transportation system, traveling to nighttime establishments in LA is easy and affordable.

West Hollywood along Santa Monica Boulevard and the Sunset Strip is one of the best places to enjoy after the day is over. Visitors can catch something to eat and live bands at several establishments in the area.

Hollywood is also hopping in the evening hours with hot nightclubs like Avalon and the '70s-themed Good Times at Davey Wayne's. On a budget? Check out Best Western's late-night diner 101 Coffee Shop.

You can also head to Koreatown for more fun. If karaoke is on the agenda, head to Brass Monkey or visit Beer Belly for a fantastic array of craft beer.

Whatever the night calls for, you can find it in Los Angeles. From beaches that are open until sunset to dance parties that go well into the night, the fun never stops.

Black Market Liquor Bar

Black Market Liquor Bar offers a unique dining experience by world-renowned executive chef Antonia Lofaso. From the leather booths to the

warm ambiance of the candle-lit tables, you won't soon forget an evening at Black Market Liquor Bar.

Reservations at Black Market Liquor Bar are not required but are highly recommended. Black Market Liquor Bar staff will accept reservations for parties of up to six people online, through email, or by phone.

The décor at Black Market Liquor Bar features a tiered and mirrored bar and a half-dome exposed brick ceiling. Be sure to try their extensive cocktail options and bite-size foods like Korean BBQ Wings, dill potato chips, and deviled quail eggs. Whether your palate is craving fish, pasta, or an amazing dessert, Black Market Liquor Bar has something for everyone.

Best Time to Visit: Black Market Liquor Bar is open Monday through Friday from 5:00 p.m. to 10:00 p.m., Saturday from 5:00 p.m. to 11:00 p.m., and Sunday from 11:00 a.m. to 3:00 p.m. and again from 5:00 p.m. to 10:00 p.m.

Pass/Permit/Fees: Valet parking is available during dinner and brunch hours for a fee. Additional parking is also available.

Physical Address:
Black Market Liquor Bar
11915 Ventura Boulevard
Los Angeles, CA 91604

GPS Coordinates: 34.14327° N, 118.39085° W

Did You Know? Antonia Lofaso owns three restaurants in Los Angeles. In the cooking community, she is known as the Warrior Princess.

Saddle Ranch Chop House

Saddle Ranch Chop House was established in 1999. One of the fun things about Saddle Ranch Chop House is the chance to try your hand at the mechanical bull.

When visiting, guests might recognize the restaurant from shows such as *Sex and the City, Desperate Housewives, Rock of Love*, and more. The staff was even featured in the 2011 VH1 reality show *Saddle Ranch*.

Aside from giving guests a chance to make it eight seconds on the bull, the Saddle Ranch Chop House offers an eclectic array of food and cocktails in a saloon-style atmosphere. Visitors will enjoy the fun Western vibe of the Saddle Ranch Chop House.

Don't forget to save room to make your own s'mores at the fire pit while enjoying the wooden and stone rustic buildings surrounding the interior walls.

Best Time to Visit: Saddle Ranch Chop House is open Monday through Friday from 4:00 p.m. to 2:00 a.m., Saturday from 10:30 a.m. to 2:00 a.m., and Sunday from 10:00 a.m. to 2:00 a.m.

Pass/Permit/Fees: Parking is available on site.

Physical Address:
Saddle Ranch Chop House
8371 Sunset Boulevard
West Hollywood, CA 90069

GPS Coordinates: 34.09585° N, 118.37233° W

Did You Know? The Houston Livestock Show and Rodeo is considered the largest rodeo in the world. It lasts 20 days, bringing in over 2 million fans annually.

Lilly Rose

Lilly Rose is a step onto the wild side tucked in an underground bar in downtown LA. Located in the basement of the Wayfair Hotel, Lilly Rose is an adventure to be remembered. Visitors can enjoy fantastic cocktails while watching live music, taking in a magic show, or enjoying burlesque entertainment.

The Looking Glass Tea Service is among the best things to enjoy at Lilly Rose. Taking a nod from Alice in Wonderland, guests can sit and enjoy spirit-infused teas, exotic highballs, and wonderful bites of brilliantly unique and decadent food. Reservations are required for the tea service.

In addition to teas and cocktails, the dining style is casual and whimsical. When looking for a memorable experience that can't be found anywhere else, make sure to stop by Lilly Rose.

Best Time to Visit: Lilly Rose is open Wednesday through Sunday from 2:00 p.m. to 6:00 p.m. and again from 7:00 p.m. to 2:00 a.m.

Pass/Permit/Fees: Parking is available at the hotel.

Physical Address:
Lilly Rose
813 Flower Street
Los Angeles, CA 90017

GPS Coordinates: 34.04717° N, 118.26057° W

Did You Know? Not only did Lewis Carroll, the author of *Alice in Wonderland*, love making up words that can be found throughout his books, but some also think he invented an early version of *Scrabble*.

No Vacancy

No Vacancy is a wonderfully restored Victorian house that was built in 1902. It reflects the era of Prohibition, with dark wood, a red-carpeted staircase, and leather accents throughout. The home offers a variety of rooms to enjoy. There's even a hidden entrance to round out the theme.

Outside, guests can enjoy a brick-walled courtyard where jazz music, burlesque shows, and other live entertainment make the evening an adventure. Although reservations are not required, they are recommended.

The menu includes a 12-item cocktail menu that rotates for a unique experience with every visit. Considered some of the best cocktail offerings in the LA area, a visit to No Vacancy is a must.

The dress code for No Vacancy is described as "dress to impress." If it looks like sportswear, try again! Jeans are welcome with collared shirts or sweaters, and slacks and dresses are also appropriate.

Best Time to Visit: No Vacancy is open Thursday through Saturday from 8:00 p.m. to 2:00 a.m.

Pass/Permit/Fees: There is no cover charge for entry.

Physical Address:
No Vacancy (in Hotel Juniper)
1727 N. Hudson Avenue
Los Angeles, CA 90028

GPS Coordinates: 34.04717° N, 118.26057° W

Did You Know? Gothic novels were at their peak during the Victorian era. Favorite works included *Dracula* and stories by Edgar Allan Poe.

Station 1640

Station 1640 provides an opportunity to dance the night away while enjoying cocktails and appetizers, including chicken wings marinated in liquor-infused sauces.

The award-winning audio, video, and lighting are perfect for live shows and events where the goal is to have fun. Station 1640 has a unique space that transforms with the event. From DJs to live music to dancing, visitors will enjoy over 4,000 square feet indoors and 3,000 square feet outdoors.

Station 1640 has a 9-foot LED display wall, 8 big-screen TVs, VIP seating, a full kitchen, and custom neon artwork that makes the venue truly shine. When visiting, check out their online events page to know what to expect. Monday is for karaoke, while Wednesday is for house and techno music. Thursday is all about the bass and drums. The weekends flow from pop and the 2000s to afro beats to reggae.

Best Time to Visit: Station 1640 is open Monday through Friday from 9:00 p.m. to 2:00 a.m. and weekends from 3:00 p.m. to 2:00 a.m.

Pass/Permit/Fees: Parking is available in the on-site lot and a nearby garage.

Physical Address:
Station 1640
1640 N. Cahuenga Boulevard
Los Angeles, CA 90028

GPS Coordinates: 34.10122° N, 118.32942° W

Did You Know? Jimmy Savile is known for hosting the world's first DJ dance party in 1943.

The Continental Club

The Continental Club offers craft cocktails, intimate moments, and ambiance, making it a must-see stop in Los Angeles. Visitors can enjoy themed nights and special events offered several nights a week.

Table service is available Thursday, Friday, and Saturday. Options include pitchers or punch for up to eight people or champagne. Reservations need to be confirmed before 6:00 p.m. Guests are encouraged to check their confirmation to understand the reservation policy. Dress code is stylish attire.

The Continental Club offers comfortable leather bench seating. The red and black décor is dramatic yet inviting.

Best Time to Visit: The Continental Club is open Wednesday from 10:00 p.m. to 2:00 a.m., Thursday from 7:00 p.m. to 2:00 a.m., and weekends from 9:00 p.m. to 2:00 a.m.

Pass/Permit/Fees: Valet parking is $15 per car. There is typically only a cover charge during special events.

Physical Address:
The Continental Club
116 4th Street
Los Angeles, CA 90013

GPS Coordinates: 34.04863° N, 118.24790° W

Did You Know? They are six main cocktails: old fashioned, martini, daiquiri, sidecar, whiskey highball, and flip.

Mondrian's Skybar

Mondrian's Skybar is an oasis in the clouds, surrounded by ivy and lush décor. Guests can lounge on daybeds or relax in the pool while enjoying cocktails from the rooftop bar. This spot boasts some of the best views in Los Angeles.

Visitors can order creative and signature cocktails, including frozen cocktails or specialty punch bowls. You can also enjoy typical bar bites like flatbreads, street tacos, and more. During the day, guests lounge poolside on wicker and teak furniture surrounded by a floral landscape perfect for soaking up the sun. In the evening, Mondrian's Skybar becomes a world-class dance club with DJs and dancing.

No reservations are needed at Mondrian's Skybar, but booking a daybed or room at the hotel is suggested if traveling with a large group. During the week, the crowd is quieter than on the weekends, but be prepared to wait for entry no matter when you arrive.

Best Time to Visit: Mondrian's Skybar is open Sunday through Thursday from 11:00 a.m. to 11:00 p.m. and Friday and Saturday from 11:00 a.m. to 2:00 a.m.

Pass/Permit/Fees: Valet and garage parking are available for $10 to $15. There is a cover charge, but the cost varies depending on the night and the evening's entertainment.

Physical Address:
Mondrian's Skybar
8440 Sunset Boulevard
West Hollywood, CA 90069

GPS Coordinates: 34.09483° N, 118.37453° W

Did You Know? The highest rooftop bar in the world is Ozone at The Ritz-Carlton in Hong Kong.

Tiki-Ti

Tiki-Ti is a Polynesian-style bar in the Los Feliz neighborhood of Los Angeles that first opened in 1961. The Tiki-Ti is the place to stop before heading to the clubs for the night.

Visitors to the Tiki-Ti are in for a treat when it comes to drinks, as the menu includes over 90 distinctive beverages. Many of them are original to the Tiki-Ti. For customers who can't decide, there is a wheel to spin to help pick out a drink.

The Tiki-Ti is decorated with items that have been donated throughout the years and a board with regulars' names on it. When visiting the Tiki-Ti, be prepared to stay inside once there. Due to the lines and how busy the bar can get, the policy doesn't allow visitors to go in and out.

Best Time to Visit: Tiki-Ti is open Wednesday through Saturday from 4:00 p.m. to 2:00 a.m.

Pass/Permit/Fees: Street parking is available with only a short walk to the bar. The cover charge depends on the day and event. There is an ATM available at the bar.

Physical Address:
Tiki-Ti
4427 Sunset Boulevard
Los Angeles, CA 90027

GPS Coordinates: 34.09767° N, 118.28580° W

Did You Know? Mixologists are often considered the chefs of drink rather than food. The study of mixing drinks is called mixology.

Black Rabbit Rose

From mystical cocktails to the wonder of magic around every corner, there is something for everyone to enjoy at Black Rabbit Rose. While visiting, you'll find a fantastic menu in the lounge offered by Crying Tiger. The menu is a wonderful mix of Thai and Chinese cuisine. Cocktails are served with the same sense of magic surrounding the entire establishment.

After eating and enjoying cocktails, guests are encouraged to attend the Black Rabbit Rose Magic Show. The small, intimate theater tucked away in the Black Rabbit Rose is the perfect spot to unwind and enjoy a night of wonder.

Magic shows typically last under an hour, and they're restricted to guests over the age of 21. The dress code for the magic shows is considered upscale. To gain an even more magical experience, make a reservation and enjoy a pre- or post-show dinner in the lounge.

Best Time to Visit: Black Rabbit Rose Lounge is open Tuesday through Saturday from 6:00 p.m. to 2:00 am. Magic shows run from Thursday to Saturday at various times.

Pass/Permit/Fees: Street parking is available. Reservations are recommended, but walk-ins are welcome. Magic show tickets start at $49.

Physical Address:
Black Rabbit Rose
1719 N. Hudson Avenue
Los Angeles, CA 90028

GPS Coordinates: 34.10201° N, 118.33214° W

Did You Know? It is thought that Louis Comte invented the rabbit-in-the-hat trick in 1814.

The Varnish

The Varnish bar opened in 2009 when Los Angeles was coming into its own in the cocktail scene. Immediately, The Varnish earned the Spirited Awards' Best American Bar and was added to the World's Best Bars List. Visitors to The Varnish might be confused since it's necessary to walk through Cole's, a traditional Irish pub, to get to The Varnish. Its hidden locale adds to the mysticism of the dark and moody speakeasy.

The Varnish does not accept reservations. Since the establishment is on the must-do list for Los Angeles, consider arriving early to get a seat. Tables receive full-service attention, but you also have the option to stand depending on your needs. Be mindful that parties of six or more cannot be seated at a table.

The Varnish doesn't have a happy hour, but guests are welcome to participate in Cole's happy-hour offerings. The Varnish serves classic cocktails in addition to its selections of beer and wine. Bite-size snacks are also available.

Best Time to Visit: The Varnish is open every day from 7:00 p.m. to 2:00 a.m.

Pass/Permit/Fees: A public parking garage is located near The Varnish. Street parking is also available after 6:00 p.m. There is no cover charge.

Physical Address:
The Varnish
118 E. 6th Street
Los Angeles, CA 90014

GPS Coordinates: 34.04497° N, 118.24950° W

Did You Know? To get to The Varnish, guests pass through Cole's, which opened in 1908. It's the longest continuously operating restaurant and pub in Los Angeles.

Parks

Los Angeles has an amazing array of parks and nature trails that are free to enjoy. Many of these parks contain some of the best landmarks to visit as well.

Consider Griffith Park, with the Griffith Observatory and Bronson Caves, or Kenneth Hahn State Recreation Area, with a gorgeous lotus pond and over seven miles of hiking and walking trails. Some of the best-kept secrets are in Los Angeles parks.

In many parks, you can spend an entire day enjoying the grounds. In all, Los Angeles has 181 parks with nearly 60 trails to explore. Be sure to check weather conditions and details for each park before visiting.

Additionally, check out rental options for the parks, as many offer bicycle or paddleboat rentals. Some even have boat tours to enjoy. When hiking, consider searching online for the difficult rating. Los Angeles county offers maps, difficulty ratings, and tips for each of the trails in the county.

Echo Park

Echo Park offers a wide variety of activities, including pedal boats and walking trails. You can also enjoy a meal at one of many picnic tables or visit nearby sites by renting a swan boat. Being out on the water is particularly enjoyable when the boats are lit up at night. The lotus flower garden and fountain are also must-see attractions when stopping by.

Echo Park is located in the neighborhood of the same name, home of the Los Angeles Dodgers. One of the first things visitors will notice as they enter the neighborhood is the colorful murals, including one behind the Bob Baker Marionette Theater that was created by over 20 local artists.

On the way to the park, stop to walk around and see how many murals you can find or visit local shops that are unique to the neighborhood. Echo Park Time Travel Mart allows shoppers to "time travel" while finding eclectic items.

Best Time to Visit: Echo Park is open to the public Monday through Friday from 10:00 a.m. to 9:00 p.m. and Saturday from 9:00 a.m. to 5:00 p.m.

Pass/Permit/Fees: There is no fee to visit the park. Rental costs for pedal boats and swan boats vary.

Physical Address:
Echo Park
1632 Bellevue Avenue
Los Angeles, CA 90026

GPS Coordinates: 34.07691° N, 118.25956° W

Did You Know? Carroll Avenue in the Echo Park neighborhood is home to many Victorian manors that have been featured in various television shows, music videos, and movies.

Descanso Gardens

Descanso Gardens is a 150-acre botanical garden featuring a wide selection of fruit trees, forested areas, and ponds for visitors to enjoy. The property was once the site of a 22-room mansion. Descanso Gardens was placed on the National Register of Historic Places in 2021.

The mansion, also known as The Boddy House, has been renovated several times and now serves as an integral part of Descanso Gardens. Visitors can take a tour inside the house and see the Sturt Haaga Gallery. The gallery educates guests about botany, horticulture, and the study of gardens and how they affect culture.

A train also runs through Descanso Gardens, offering another view of the wonderful landscape. You can even enjoy a meal at The Kitchen during your visit. The menu features fresh local produce.

Best Time to Visit: Descanso Gardens is open every day from 9:00 a.m. to 5:00 p.m. Visitors can book a free ticket in advance for entry on the third Tuesday of every month. This deal does not apply at the door.

Pass/Permit/Fees: Admission costs $15 for adults, $11 for seniors or students, and $5 for children over 13. Children 12 and under may visit for free. Train tickets are an additional $5.

Physical Address:
Descanso Gardens
1418 Descanso Drive
La Cañada Flintridge, CA 91011

GPS Coordinates: 34.20116° N, 118.21189° W

Did You Know? The property overlooks the San Gabriel Mountains, home to the Mount Wilson Observatory.

Griffith Park

With over 4,511 acres, Griffith Park is one of the largest municipal parks in the United States even after including urban wilderness areas.

Visitors to Griffith Park can easily stay the entire day enjoying the Los Angeles Zoo, the Griffith Observatory, and more.

Inside the park, bicycle rentals are available, as well as pony and train rides. Enjoy Fern Dell, which showcases over 50 ferns nestled among a trail that winds through the park. Bronson Caves is another must-see when visiting.

Guests who want to enjoy a piece of history can visit the Autry Museum of the American West or the Los Angeles Live Steamers Railroad Museum. This is in addition to walking through the park and enjoying over 150 plant species.

Best Time to Visit: The park is open daily from 5:00 a.m. to 10:30 p.m., but each attraction within the park has its own hours of operation.

Pass/Permit/Fees: Entrance to the park is free. Attractions within the park may have a separate admission fee.

Physical Address:
Griffith Park
4730 Crystal Springs Drive
Los Angeles, CA 90027

GPS Coordinates: 34.13676° N, 118.29420° W

Did You Know? There are roughly 200 operating steam trains in the United States. The first one, the Stourbridge Lion, started operating in 1829.

Grand Park

Grand Park is a 12-acre park designed to connect the neighborhood of Bunker Hill to the Los Angeles Civic Center. It boasts an interactive fountain plaza, shaded sidewalks, and year-round family-friendly events.

Visitors to the park can enjoy the water activities, including a wading pool, a fountain, and splash pads. There are many lawns and picnic tables dotted throughout the park for a place to relax or have a meal. The park is accessible thanks to ramps, sloped walks, and an elevator that allows all guests to enjoy the lush greenery and plants.

Grand Park is the place to visit for New Year's Eve, as it features a light projection show, food trucks, and live music. Many other concerts take place in the park as well. Be sure to check out the park website to find out what events are happening during your planned visit.

Alcohol, drones, fires, and entering the fountains are just some of the things not allowed at Grand Park. In addition, if traveling with four-legged friends, make sure to keep them on a leash.

Best Time to Visit: The park is open daily from 5:30 a.m. to 10:00.

Pass/Permit/Fees: The park is free to visit.

Physical Address:
Grand Park
200 N. Grand Avenue
Los Angeles, CA 90012

GPS Coordinates: 34.05581° N, 118.24575° W

Did You Know? The first New Year's Eve celebration dates back more than 4,000 years when Julius Caesar declared the day a national holiday.

Palisades Park

Palisades Park boasts more than 30 species of plants and trees and a variety of art and historic features, including a Civil War cannon from 1908. With fantastic views of Santa Monica Bay, Palisades Park is a wonderful place to stop and enjoy the Los Angeles weather. With 26 acres along Ocean Avenue, the park provides a calm place to sit, watch the water, or feel the breeze on a warm day.

Palisades Park offers benches for visitors to relax on while taking a break from the walking path. Guests can also enjoy a meal at one of many picnic tables. Locals say that on a clear day, it's easy to see Malibu from the park.

While visiting, enjoy the surrounding neighborhood, including a stop at Santa Monica Pier or a walk down Third Street Promenade. Santa Monica is also home to street performers, public art, and a wide variety of unique shopping opportunities.

Guests should note that the Palisades Bluffs are off limits while visiting the park. Parking can be found in metered lots and nearby parking garages.

Best Time to Visit: The park is open daily from 5:00 a.m. to 12:00 a.m.

Pass/Permit/Fees: There is no fee to enjoy the park.

Physical Address:
Pacific Palisades
851 Alma Real Drive
Pacific Palisades, CA 90272

GPS Coordinates: 34.04237° N, 118.52439° W

Did You Know? Los Angeles County manages 20 beaches that run along 26 miles of coastland.

Museums & Galleries

With its deep history of culture and entertainment, Los Angeles features a wide variety of museums and galleries to explore. An updated list shows more than 90 museums offering exhibits that range from historical to kid friendly. If art galleries are in your vacation plans, the options more than double since there are more than 190 in the area.

Guides to museums and galleries can be found online. Additionally, check out the locations of each one, as many are close to other attractions that might be attractive to your group.

Some of the best museums and galleries to visit are The Getty Center, the Los Angeles County Museum of Art, Huntington Library, and La Brea Tar Pits and Museum. Each of these is detailed further in this guide.

Huntington Library, Art Museum, and Botanical Gardens

The Huntington is a fantastic stop during any Los Angeles vacation. Visitors can view rare books, beautiful gardens, or fabulous art in one area across the 207-acre complex.

You should plan to spend more than three hours enjoying all The Huntington has to offer. It's important to make a reservation as capacity is limited. During the weekend, reservations are required.

The Huntington offers various tours for guests. Specialty and group tours require reservations and start at $34 for the group option. Free tours are also available with general admission or membership. These tours do not require reservations, but they're not available on Tuesday or days with free admission. The Huntington offers a digital guide to the property that you can download during your visit.

Best Time to Visit: The Huntington is open Wednesday through Monday from 10:00 a.m. to 5:00 p.m.

Pass/Permit/Fees: Admission costs $25 for adults during the week and $29 on the weekends. Children ages 4 to 11 cost $13 regardless of the day, and children under 4 may visit for free.

Physical Address:
The Huntington Library, Art Museum, and Botanical Gardens
1151 Oxford Road
San Marino, CA 91108

GPS Coordinates: 34.12922° N, 118.11452° W

Did You Know? The Huntington Library has a collection of more than 8,000 miniature books that are each the size of a silver dollar.

Academy Museum of Motion Picture

The Academy Museum of Motion Picture is the perfect place to visit if you're a movie buff. The museum is home to more than 13 million movie artifacts, from costumes to props, dating back to 1927.

Timed admission tickets grant access to four full floors of memorabilia, two theaters, and a restaurant. There's even an interactive display that lets visitors accept their own Academy Award onstage. Plan to spend anywhere from three to four hours enjoying iconic movie moments.

Tickets can be purchased in advance for general admission and special events or exhibitions. Visitor Experience Associates are located throughout the museum to provide any assistance needed. Flash photography is not permitted, nor are tripods, monopods, or selfie sticks. There are posted areas where photography is not allowed.

Best Time to Visit: The Academy Museum of Motion Picture is open Sunday through Thursday from 10:00 a.m. to 6:00 p.m. as well as Friday and Saturday from 10:00 a.m. to 8:00 p.m.

Pass/Permit/Fees: Admission costs $25 for adults, $19 for seniors, and $15 for students. Children younger than 17 may visit for free.

Physical Address:
Academy Museum of Motion Pictures
6067 Wilshire Boulevard
Los Angeles, CA 90036

GPS Coordinates: 34.06362° N, 118.36085° W

Did You Know? The first Academy Awards ceremony was held in 1929 at the Hollywood Roosevelt Hotel.

The Getty

The J. Paul Getty Museum, or simply "The Getty" for short, opened in 1974 in the Brentwood neighborhood of Los Angeles. The Getty art museum features paintings, sculptures, photographs, and more from all over the world.

The courtyard at The Getty is the perfect spot to sit and visit while enjoying the fountains and something to eat or drink. Additionally, a trip through the Central Garden will provide a sense of peace thanks to tranquil water features and lush landscaping.

Inside, guests can spend up to three hours walking through exhibits featuring topics from Van Gogh to modern art. To enhance the experience, be sure to download The Getty app for an in-depth look at what the museum offers. When using the app, bring earbuds to avoid interrupting other guests.

Best Time to Visit: The Getty is open Tuesday through Friday and again on Sunday from 10:00 a.m. to 5:30 p.m. On Saturday, it is open from 10:00 a.m. to 8:00 p.m.

Pass/Permit/Fees: Admission is free, but parking is $20 per car or motorcycle. After 3:00 p.m., parking is discounted to $15. For evening events or on Saturday after 6:00 p.m., parking is $10. Entry is timed for an adequate flow of visitors.

Physical Address:
The J. Paul Getty Museum
1200 Getty Center Drive
Los Angeles, CA 90049

GPS Coordinates: 34.07821° N, 118.47412° W

Did You Know? The Metropolitan Museum of Art in New York City is the largest art museum in the United States.

Los Angeles County
Museum of Art

The Los Angeles County Museum of Art is the largest museum in the western part of the United States, featuring more than 150,000 pieces of art. The museum is located in Hancock Park and spreads over 20 acres.

Although walk-up tickets are available, admission is timed and some time slots sell out. For guaranteed entry, be sure to buy advanced tickets. All visitors must pass a health screening upon entry, and masks are encouraged. Plan to arrive 10–15 minutes before your ticketed time

General admission tickets are good for the entire museum, and you should plan to spend at least two hours. Dining is available at two restaurants. One is a full-service restaurant that encourages reservations, while the other offers lighter options.

Best Time to Visit: The Los Angeles County Museum of Art is open Monday, Tuesday, and Thursday from 11:00 a.m. to 6:00 p.m., Friday from 11:00 a.m. to 8:00 p.m., and weekends from 10:00 a.m. to 7:00 p.m.

Pass/Permit/Fees: For those who live outside Los Angeles County, tickets range from $10 to $25, and children 2 and under are free. Nearby parking is available at the Pritzker Parking Garage for $20. Discounted prices are available for residents of Los Angeles County.

Physical Address:
Los Angeles County Museum of Art
5905 Wilshire Boulevard
Los Angeles, CA 90036

GPS Coordinates: 34.06407° N, 118.35925° W

Did You Know? The *Mona Lisa* is considered the most famous painting in the world. It was painted in the 1500s by Leonardo da Vinci.

Natural History Museum

The Natural History Museum of Los Angeles County is the largest of its kind in this region of the country. The museum opened in 1913 as the Museum of History, Science, and Art but split from the art museum in 1961.

The museum has three floors of permanent exhibits that range from animal habitats and dinosaurs to an insect zoo. In the spring and summer, guests can enjoy a butterfly pavilion. That same area focuses on spiders in the fall.

Visitors can enjoy over 240 specimens in the Dino Lab, while more than 2,000 gems and minerals sparkle in the Gem and Mineral Hall. Plan to spend more than three hours in the Natural History Museum, exploring a mix of exhibits and shows.

Purchasing tickets in advance is recommended to ensure entry. Dining options are available in the Neighborhood Grill.

Best Time to Visit: The Natural History Museum is open every day from 9:30 a.m. to 5:00 p.m.

Pass/Permit/Fees: Admission costs $15 for adults, $12 for seniors or students, and $7 for children. The *Dinosaur Encounters* exhibit costs an additional $6.

Physical Address:
Natural History Museum of Los Angeles County
900 Exposition Boulevard
Los Angeles, CA 90007

GPS Coordinates: 34.01731° N, 118.28862° W

Did You Know? The *Spinosaurus* is the biggest carnivore ever recorded, reaching a length of 50 feet and a weight of 7.5 tons.

California Science Center

The California Science Center is next to the Natural History Museum of Los Angeles County. The museum features a 2-story, 45,000-square-foot ecosystems display and space exhibits that include the space shuttle *Endeavour*. You can photograph exhibits, but flash photography is prohibited inside special exhibits. Signs are posted for further information.

Plan to spend anywhere from two to three hours enjoying the museum. With over 100 permanent and interactive exhibits and galleries, everyone in the group should be able to find something to enjoy. If traveling with guests under age seven, check out the Discovery Rooms for a unique take on science that's just their size.

Best Time to Visit: The California Science Center is open every day from 10:00 a.m. to 5:00 p.m.

Pass/Permit/Fees: There is no cost to view the permanent galleries. Timed tickets must be purchased online in advance for any events in the IMAX theater.

Physical Address:
California Science Center
700 Exposition Park Drive
Los Angeles, CA 90037

GPS Coordinates: 34.01505° N, 118.28583° W

Did You Know? Six space missions have landed on the moon since 1969. The first mission included Neil Armstrong walking on the moon.

GRAMMY Museum

The GRAMMY Museum is an interactive experience for anyone passionate about music and entertainers. There are 4 floors loaded with memorabilia, as well as a 200-seat theater. In all, more than 400 items are on display.

The GRAMMY Museum opened in 2008. It includes exhibits from all aspects of music, including many interactive features such as touring recording booths and creating their own tracks.

You should expect to spend one to two hours in the museum. Guided tours are available for an in-depth look at the museum's exhibits.

Best Time to Visit: The GRAMMY Museum is open Wednesday through Friday, Sunday, and Monday from 11:00 a.m. to 5:00 p.m. On Saturday, hours are from 10:00 a.m. to 6:00 p.m.

Pass/Permit/Fees: Admission is $18 for adults, $15 for seniors or students, $12 for children 6 and up, and free for children under 5. Tickets must be purchased online. They are not available on site.

Physical Address:
GRAMMY Museum
800 W. Olympic Boulevard
Los Angeles, CA 90015

GPS Coordinates: 34.04485° N, 118.26464° W

Did You Know? According to *Guinness World Records*, the most popular song of all time is "White Christmas" by Irving Berlin.

Autry Museum of the American West

The Autry Museum of the American West offers a unique look into the history, art, and culture of the region. It was founded in 1988 by Gene Autry and houses over 500,000 pieces in addition to lectures, events, and live music.

Popular attractions include the full-size chuck wagon in the Cowboy Gallery and the *Human Nature* exhibit that focuses on how culture and ecology have changed the California landscape. The Autry Museum of the American West also offers several programming events each month, from *Family Play Space* to *Music Showcase*.

Best Time to Visit: The Autry Museum of the American West is open Tuesday through Sunday from 10:00 a.m. to 4:00 p.m.

Pass/Permit/Fees: Admission is $16 for adults, $12 for students or seniors, $8 for children 3 and up, and free for children under 3.

Physical Address:
Autry Museum of the American West
Griffith Park
4700 Western Heritage Way
Los Angeles, CA 90027

GPS Coordinates: 34.14880° N, 118.28125° W

Did You Know? Most people think about horses when they think about the American West, but in 1856, the U.S. Camel Corps was established as an experiment for the United States Army.

The Broad

The Broad is a 120,000-square-foot building featuring more than 2,000 postwar and contemporary artworks. The museum has two floors and is also home to The Broad Art Foundation's lending museum, which loans collections to museums worldwide. The Broad opened in 2015.

No food or beverage is permitted inside the museum. Additionally, no bags larger than 11 x 17 x 8 inches will be allowed inside. There is a mobile museum guide available to enhance your visit, so be sure to bring your headphones.

Families are welcome at The Broad and encouraged to use the available Kid's Audio Tour hosted by LeVar Burton to tour the museum. Strollers are allowed as well.

Best Time to Visit: The Broad is open Tuesday, Wednesday, and Friday from 11:00 a.m. to 5:00 p.m. The Broad is also open from 10:00 a.m. to 6:00 p.m. on weekends.

Pass/Permit/Fees: The Broad has an underground parking facility for visitors. Parking is $17 for the first 3 hours and $5 for each additional 15 minutes. The daily maximum is $27. Admission is free, but some exhibits might carry a separate charge. Tickets must be reserved online. All tickets are timed.

Physical Address:
The Broad
221 S. Grand Avenue
Los Angeles, CA 90012

GPS Coordinates: 34.0545° N, 118.2502° W

Did You Know? The Wadsworth Atheneum Museum of Art is the oldest public art museum in the United States. It opened in 1842.

Famous Buildings
& Structures

Many of the country's most famous buildings and structures are in Los Angeles. Along with amazing architecture and fascinating history, a tour of iconic attractions is a wonderful way to spend a vacation.

For example, Watts Towers is a collection of 17 sculptures that are almost 100 feet tall. Made of metal and concrete, the sculpture was built by hand over 33 years. The towers are listed on the National Register of Historic Places. They can be found in Simon Rodia State Park.

The Eastern Columbia Building located in downtown LA is an Art Deco wonder with a teal terracotta exterior embellished with golden chevrons and sunbursts. The building offers upscale shopping on the ground floor and gorgeous lines for pictures.

Hollywood Bowl opened in 1922 and has offered live entertainment in a gorgeous setting for over 100 years. It has an extensive calendar of events for visitors to enjoy, as well as world-class dining from James Beard award-winning chef Suzanne Goin. Picnicking is also an option at Hollywood Bowl. Reserve spots and order picnic boxes in advance.

TCL Chinese Theatre

Originally known as Grauman's Chinese Theatre, the TCL Chinese Theatre is a historic landmark in Los Angeles. The original theatre opened in 1927 with a showing of *The King of Kings*. Since then, the theatre has undergone many changes, but the importance of the building and the iconic handprints in concrete outside its door remain.

Visitors to the TCL Chinese Theatre can enjoy an IMAX movie in an auditorium that offers state-of-the-art cinema technology and immersive audio. While there, join a theatre tour to learn more about its history, and don't forget to spend time checking out some of the industry's biggest names on the sidewalk outside. There are nearly 200 handprints in the concrete at the TCL Chinese Theatre. The tradition started in 1927. Besides handprints, you'll be able to see imprints of the wands used in Harry Potter, a cigar from Groucho Marx, and hoofprints from Gene Autry's horse.

Best Time to Visit: A schedule of showtimes can be found online. VIP tours are offered seven days a week, excluding special event days.

Pass/Permit/Fees: Tours and movie prices vary. There is no cost to see the handprints outside the building.

Physical Address:
TCL Chinese Theatre
6925 Hollywood Boulevard
Hollywood, CA 90028

GPS Coordinates: 34.10217° N, 118.34104° W

Did You Know? The tradition of adding imprints to the concrete outside the theatre started as an accident when silent film star Norma Talmadge accidentally stepped into the wet cement. That gave the owners the idea, and the rest is history.

Griffith Observatory

Griffith Observatory is in Griffith Park. It originally opened in 1935, and it offers a fascinating view of the Los Angeles basin, including the iconic Hollywood sign. While visiting Griffith Park, take the time to tour the observatory and its nearly 60 exhibits. You can also use the free telescopes to see more of the area.

Griffith Observatory is home to the Samuel Oschin Planetarium. Visitors can enjoy daily programs in the planetarium such as the live Tesla coil demonstration. The Zeiss Mark IV Star Projector another popular attraction.

Be mindful that food and drink are not allowed in the observatory. There is a café on the lower level where food and beverages can be purchased and consumed.

Best Time to Visit: The Griffith Observatory is open Tuesday through Friday from 12:00 p.m. to 10:00 p.m. and weekends from 10:00 a.m. to 10:00 p.m.

Pass/Permit/Fees: The Griffith Observatory is free to the public with paid parking nearby.

Physical Address:
Griffith Observatory
2800 E. Observatory Road
Los Angeles, CA 90027

GPS Coordinates: 34.11918° N, 118.30034° W

Did You Know? There are 88 official constellations. The first constellation recorded was Taurus the Bull.

Capitol Records Building

The Capital Records Building was designed to look like a stack of records, and it's home to some of history's most famous musical artists. The 13-story tower in Hollywood was completed in 1956.

The building is not open to the public, but it's worth a stop when in Los Angeles. It's only a short walk from the Hollywood Walk of Fame, so take a minute to snap a picture of your group outside the building and imagine the stars who have stood in the same spot. Several tours of Hollywood go by the building as well, providing a history of the building and Capital Studios.

Besides the Hollywood Walk of Fame, nearby attractions include Hollywood Boulevard, the TCL Chinese Theatre, and the Hollywood Pantages Theatre.

Best Time to Visit: If visiting the building after dark, take note of the flashing light on top that spells out *Hollywood* in Morse code.

Pass/Permit/Fees: The building is not open to the public, but there's no fee to visit the outside.

Physical Address:
Capitol Records Building
1750 Vine Street
Los Angeles, CA 90028

GPS Coordinates: 34.10340° N, 118.32642° W

Did You Know? Columbia Records is the oldest record company in the United States.

Hollyhock House

The Aline Barnsdall Hollyhock House in East Hollywood was designed by Frank Lloyd Wright. It is now the centerpiece of Barnsdall Art Park.

Both virtual and in-person tours are available for the Hollyhock House. Advance tickets are required for in-person tours. Self-guided tours allow guests to see the house at their own speed, and docents are available to answer questions. Guidebooks are also available on site.

Food and drink are not permitted in the house, but guests can enjoy a picnic in Barnsdall Art Park. When visiting, be mindful that flat or broad-heeled shoes are required. Additionally, strollers are not allowed in the home.

The Hollyhock House is one of 400 remaining homes designed by Frank Lloyd Wright. In all, he designed more than 1,000 homes, office buildings, and other structures.

Best Time to Visit: Hollyhock House is open Thursday through Saturday from 11:00 a.m. to 4:00 p.m.

Pass/Permit/Fees: Self-guided tour tickets are $7 for adults, $3 for seniors over 65, and $3 for students with ID. Children under 12 may visit for free and should be accompanied by an adult.

Physical Address:
Hollyhock House
4800 Hollywood Boulevard
Los Angeles, CA 90027

GPS Coordinates: 34.10013° N, 118.29440° W

Did You Know? In addition to being an architect, Frank Lloyd Wright was a teacher and a writer. There are 20 books published under his name.

The Gamble House

The Gamble House is a marvel of architecture designed in the American Arts and Crafts style. Architects Charles and Henry Greene designed the home and furnishings in 1908. The home was designed for David and Mary Gamble of the Proctor & Gamble Company.

A tour of the home typically takes one to two hours depending on the chosen tour. Options are a one-hour docent-guided tour, the Behind the Velvet Ropes Tour, and the Details & Joinery Tour that looks at the craftsmanship of the home. Other tours offer a look at the grounds and the neighborhood.

Food and beverages are not allowed in the house. When traveling with children, be mindful that strollers are not permitted inside. It is important to wear flat or broad-heeled shoes to minimize the risk of damage to the floors. You must also avoid leaning on the furniture or touching items in the house without docents' permission.

Best Time to Visit: The Gamble House is open Friday and Sunday from 12:00 p.m. to 3:00 p.m., Saturday from 11:30 a.m. to 3:00 p.m., and Tuesday and Thursday from 11:15 a.m. to 3:00 p.m.

Pass/Permit/Fees: There is parking in front of the Gamble House and on Westmoreland Place.

Physical Address:
The Gamble House
4 Westmoreland Place
Pasadena, CA 91103

GPS Coordinates: 34.15179° N, 118.16095° W

Did You Know? Arts and Crafts–style homes take inspiration from nature with simple forms and patterns.

Gardens

Although Los Angeles is a large, expansive city, plenty of green spots remain nearby. There are many botanical gardens and floral fields throughout LA and the neighboring areas, both big and small. Plants indigenous to California and imported from worldwide are found in these vibrant green settings.

In fact, Los Angeles has some of the best gardens in the nation. From Japanese and botanical gardens to arboretums full of lush trees, beauty is all around when visiting one of these amazing spots.

Consider taking a trip out to Arlington Garden in Pasadena. This three-acre botanical garden is free to the public and maintained by the community. It has a wonderful citrus grove, benches for seating, and oak trees to provide shade. Arlington Garden is open seven days a week.

Greystone Mansion is a study in topiary. The Tudor Revival mansion with English gardens is owned by the city of Beverly Hills. It is a public park with free access to stroll the grounds and appreciate the lush landscaping.

UCLA Mildred E. Mathias
Botanical Garden

The UCLA Mildred E. Mathias Botanical Garden takes up just over seven acres on the campus of UCLA. The garden was initially used for academic purposes when the campus opened in 1929, and while it's still used for education, it's now also open to the public. The UCLA Mildred E. Mathias Botanical Garden offers a varied collection of trees, plants that are native to California, and more. You'll also find a habitat garden and stream on the grounds.

Self-guided resources are available to supplement your tour through the garden. Audio tracks can be utilized in English or Spanish. Visitors can also find a map of the garden online and track their progress that way. Guided tours typically last from 45 minutes to 1 hour and offer a detailed look at the history of the botanical garden and the species that are found there. Check online for more information about guided or group tours.

Best Time to Visit: The UCLA Mildred E. Mathias Botanical Garden is open Monday through Friday from 8:00 a.m. to 4:00 p.m. and weekends from 9:00 a.m. to 4:00 p.m.

Pass/Permit/Fees: There is no cost to visit the garden.

Physical Address:
UCLA Mildred E. Mathias Botanical Garden
707 Tiverton Drive
Los Angeles, CA 90095

GPS Coordinates: 34.06678° N, 118.44153° W

Did You Know? The largest botanical garden in the world is located in Kew, south of London. It is over 300 acres wide and has 8.3 million plant specimens.

James Irvine Japanese Gardens

The James Irvine Japanese Gardens were first completed in 1980. They cover 8,500 square feet and are collectively known as the "Garden with the Clear Stream." In 1981, the gardens received a National Landscape Award from the American Association of Nurserymen. Since then, they have undergone renovations but have kept the same layout. It wasn't until 2009 that the gardens became available for private events.

The James Irvine Japanese Gardens are part of the Japanese Cultural Center in the heart of Little Tokyo. A layout of the area is available online, including a plant legend for easy identification when visiting.

Best Time to Visit: The gardens are open Tuesday through Friday from 10:00 a.m. to 5:00 p.m. and weekends from 10:00 a.m. to 5:00 p.m. Times are subject to change due to private events, and reservations are required.

Pass/Permit/Fees: The gardens are free to enjoy with a time limit of one hour.

Physical Address:
James Irvin Japanese Garden at JACCC
244 San Pedro Street
Los Angeles, CA 90012

GPS Coordinates: 34.04784° N, 118.24165° W

Did You Know? Stone, water, and plants are three essential elements of Japanese gardens.

Los Angeles River
Center & Gardens

Los Angeles River Center & Gardens is a public park located in the Cypress Park neighborhood. The area is known for its hacienda-style grounds and gorgeous landscaping.

During a tour of Los Angeles River Center & Gardens, you'll see ivy-covered walls, wrought-iron gates, and serene fountains. Many private events are held on the grounds due to their appearance of being "away from it all," even though the River Center & Gardens is only minutes away from downtown LA.

The River Garden Park has a visitor center that describes the history of the property and the Los Angeles River. It is a self-guided exhibit that only takes a few minutes to see. The center also has dioramas of flora and fauna on display, and the park itself offers hiking and picnic areas.

Best Time to Visit: The Los Angeles River Center & Garden is open Monday through Friday from 9:00 a.m. to 5:00 p.m.

Pass/Permit/Fees: There is no charge to enjoy the Los Angeles River Center & Gardens.

Physical Address:
Los Angeles River Center & Gardens
570 W. Avenue 26, #100
Los Angeles, CA 90065

GPS Coordinates: 34.08495° N, 118.22482° W

Did You Know? The concrete walls of the Los Angeles River, which no longer runs freely, have been featured in many films such as *Grease* and *Chinatown*.

South Coast Botanic Garden

South Coast Botanic Garden encompasses 87 acres in the serene setting of the Palos Verdes Hills. There are over 150,000 landscaped plants and trees in the garden as well as 300 species of birds. It is the world's first botanical garden created over a sanitary landfill.

The South Coast Botanic Garden offers an array of programming for all ages. Visitors can enjoy an old-fashioned game of hide-and-seek while looking for spectacular sculptures in the gardens. A secret sculpture map is located online.

Lectures, classes, self-guided tours, and more make the South Coast Botanic Garden a great place to stop when visiting Los Angeles. If you're traveling with children, make sure to ride the train and stop by the children's garden. You can also ride bikes, hike, and enjoy bird walks.

Best Time to Visit: South Coast Botanic Garden is open every day from 8:00 a.m. to 5:00 p.m. Tram tours are offered on weekends.

Pass/Permit/Fees: Admission is $15 for adults, $11 for seniors or students, $11 for children ages 5 to 12, and $5 for children under 5. Tram tickets are an additional $5. They can be booked through the garden office.

Physical Address:
South Coast Botanic Garden
26300 Crenshaw Boulevard
Palos Verdes Estates, CA 90274

GPS Coordinates: 33.78340° N, 118.34893° W

Did You Know? One of the largest botanical gardens in the world is located in the Bronx, NY; it boasts over 12,000 species.

Chavez Ravine Arboretum

Chavez Ravine Arboretum in Elysian Park contains more than 140 trees from around the world, including the oldest and largest Cape chestnut, Kauri, and Tipu trees in the United States. The arboretum was founded in 1893, and the first batch of trees were continuously planted until 1920.

Over the years, new saplings are each marked with metal name tags for easy management. Visitors can enjoy a picnic in the park or look for the tallest, oldest, and quirkiest trees. A map of the trees is available online for those interested in further exploring the property.

The park itself is 600 acres, offering a variety of activities in addition to the Chavez Ravine Arboretum. It is one of the oldest parts of Los Angeles. When visiting with children, take advantage of the play areas, hiking and biking paths, and spectacular city views.

Best Time to Visit: Elysian Park is open 7 days a week from 5:00 a.m. to 9:00 p.m.

Pass/Permit/Fees: Admission to the arboretum is free.

Physical Address:
Chavez Ravine Arboretum
1025 Elysian Park Drive
Los Angeles, CA 90012

GPS Coordinates: 34.08554° N, 118.24584° W

Did You Know? Arboretums are essential for conservation efforts to save endangered trees. The largest arboretum in the world is the Royal Botanic Gardens in Kew, England.

Exposition Park Rose Garden

Exposition Park Rose Garden is a sunken seven-acre garden that has been called one of the city's best-kept secrets. The garden was constructed in 1927, starting with 15,000 rose bushes.

Now, visitors to the Exposition Park Rose Garden can see more than 20,000 flowers. Over the years, many things have threatened to close the park, including digging up the garden for an underground parking structure, but the park and garden have survived.

Visitors can enjoy taking pictures of the gorgeous blooms or simply breathing in the sweet scent of roses as they walk along the path. In addition to the Rose Garden, you can stop by the California Science Center or explore the Natural History Museum of Los Angeles County while in the park. Last but not least, you can see the historic Los Angeles Memorial Coliseum among the rose bushes, providing the perfect backdrop for the beautiful landscaping.

Best Time to Visit: Exposition Park Rose Garden is open every day from 9:00 a.m. to 7:30 p.m. It closes annually between January 1st and March 15th.

Pass/Permit/Fees: Exposition Park Rose Garden is free to enjoy. Parking starts at $15.

Physical Address:
Exposition Park Rose Garden
701 State Drive
Los Angeles, CA 90037

GPS Coordinates: 34.01752° N, 118.28592° W

Did You Know? The most common is the rose, and the oldest color is the pink rose. The rarest color for roses is blue.

Amir's Garden

Amir's Garden is on the east side of Griffith Park. A one-mile hike begins at the picnic areas and arrives at Amir's Garden. Visitors will find succulents, hidden picnic tables, and tall sycamores along the way.

The five-acre volunteer garden is a great stop for hikers, horseback riders, and families looking for amazing views among nature. Don't forget to bring plenty of water, sunscreen for the hike, and a camera to document the sites. A trail map is located online to ensure safety along the way.

Amir's Garden is a unique space near the Old Zoo Picnic Area. You can walk through the area and see the old enclosures for the zoo that are now used as picnic areas. The structures were left behind when the new zoo was built in 1960 just a few miles away.

Best Time to Visit: Amir's Garden is open every day from 5:00 a.m. to 10:30 p.m.

Pass/Permit/Fees: There is no fee to enjoy Amir's Garden.

Physical Address:
Amir's Garden
Griffith Park Drive
Los Angeles, CA 90027

GPS Coordinates: 34.14248° N, 118.29291° W

Did You Know? The Philadelphia Zoo is the oldest zoo in the United States. It first opened its doors in 1874.

Beaches

California is known for its beaches, and Los Angeles has plenty of them. With over 75 miles of shoreline and 100 beaches, there is a lot of fun to be had in the sun and sand when visiting.

Los Angeles beaches are well known for their surfing. Other popular pursuits include kitesurfing, parasailing, bodyboarding, paddleboarding, and kayaking. Swimmers, snorkelers, scuba divers, and skin divers will also feel at home among the enchanting kelp forests and intriguing aquatic creatures.

The Los Angeles County lifeguards patrol the city's coast. They are not only the largest organization of professional lifeguards in the world, but they also inspired the *Baywatch* television series. Lifeguards are stationed at numerous Los Angeles beaches, including Las Tunas County Beach, Topanga County Beach, and Westward Beach (where *Baywatch* was filmed).

Long Beach

Long Beach covers a stretch of four miles from Long Beach Harbor at the Belmont Pier to Alamitos Bay. Bluff Park is connected to this beach and features a pedestrian walking path. The wide path is perfect for cyclists and walkers. Swimming is available when lifeguards are on duty. Surfing isn't the best at Long Beach since the water is protected by breakwaters constructed in the 1940s. Before that, the beach was populated by longboard surfers. Parking is available along Ocean Boulevard.

While visiting the beach, it's also convenient to head into the city. The surrounding area has excellent shopping at The Pike Outlets, or you can enjoy a day at the Aquarium of the Pacific. The Earl Burns Miller Japanese Garden is also around the corner, close to the campus of Long Beach State. If whale watching is on your agenda, check out Harbor Breeze Cruises at Rainbow Harbor for 45-minute harbor tours. In addition to whale watching, you may even see California sea lions.

Best Time to Visit: Long Beach is accessible to the public every day from 8:00 a.m. to 6:00 p.m.

Pass/Permit/Fees: Long Beach is free to visit. Parking costs vary depending on the location.

Physical Address:
Shoreline Aquatic Park
200 Aquarium Way
Long Beach, CA 90802

GPS Coordinates: 33.76036° N, 118.19511° W

Did You Know? Thanks to the constantly moving water, it can take thousands of years to form a beach.

Seal Beach

Seal Beach is the northernmost beach in Orange County. Since it's especially wide, this beach is a popular attraction for visitors and locals on warm days.

Seal Beach Municipal Pier is the longest wooden pier in the state of California. Seal Beach is also home to Eisenhower Park, a stretch of green space that is perfect for those traveling with children who want to enjoy the beach and a play area for children at the same time. Visitors can enjoy surfing, fishing, volleyball, swimming, and more, but no pets are allowed on the beach.

While in the area, stop by to take a picture of *Slick*, a bronze depiction of the California seals that used to lounge on the beach. You can even look for real seals on less populated stretches of the beach or bicycle along the San Gabriel River Bike Trail, a 28-mile stretch that ends at the San Gabriel Mountains.

Best Time to Visit: Although the beach is open daily, the Seal Beach Pier Playground is only open Wednesday through Saturday from 4:30 a.m. to 10:00 p.m.

Pass/Permit/Fees: There is no fee to enjoy Seal Beach. Parking fees vary depending on location.

Physical Address:
Seal Beach Pier Playground
900 Ocean Avenue
Seal Beach, CA 90740

GPS Coordinates: 33.73954° N, 118.10623° W

Did You Know? If you hear seals making clicking noises, they're communicating with other seals.

Santa Monica Beach

Santa Monica Beach is perhaps the most well-known beach in the Los Angeles area. With the beach and Santa Monica Pier nearby, the area offers a wide variety of activities. It's the perfect beach stop while on vacation.

The beach is over three miles long and centrally located within walking distance of many attractions and hotels. Additionally, the Annenberg Community Beach House at the north end is a nice place to relax away from the sun or watch the sunset. Parking is located nearby as well.

For families needing a break from the sand, the North Beach Playground has sensory play elements, swings, slides, and more. In the Community Beach House, a pool and splash pad are available.

Parking is also located on the south side of the shore. If you park on this end, you'll pass the Original Muscle Beach, which has gymnastics equipment, and Carousel Park.

Best Time to Visit: The beach is open from sunrise to sunset.

Pass/Permit/Fees: The beach is free to visit. Parking is available in eight main lots or on the street. Costs range from $6 to $15.

Physical Address:
Santa Monica State Beach
1150 E. Pacific Coast Highway
Santa Monica, CA 90403

GPS Coordinates: 34.01647° N, 118.50201° W

Did You Know? The oldest carousel in the United States is in Oaks Bluff, MA. The Flying Horse carousel has been in operation since 1876.

Malibu Lagoon State Beach

Malibu Lagoon State Beach is also known as Surfrider Beach. The 110-acre site is also a California state park. The beach hosted the first World Surfing Reserve in 2010.

Located along the Malibu Pier, Malibu Lagoon State Beach is best known for surfing within its three main surfing areas. It is also great for whale watching, birdwatching, and sunbathing.

Settle on the beach and relax while the waves come in, but pay attention to how close you are to the water. During optimum surfing times, it's easy to get wet if you're too close.

While at Malibu Lagoon State Beach, book a tour of the Adamson House. The tour provides a look inside the home and allows you to see a beautiful collection of Malibu pottery tiles. This historic house offers tours on Thursday, Friday, and Saturday from 11:00 a.m. to 3:00 p.m.

Best Time to Visit: Malibu Lagoon State Beach is open to the public for day use Monday through Saturday from 7:00 a.m. to 8:00 p.m. and Sunday from 7:00 a.m. to 9:30 p.m.

Pass/Permit/Fees: Entry to Malibu Lagoon State Beach is free. Parking costs depend on the lot.

Physical Address:
Malibu Lagoon State Beach
3835 Cross Creek Road
Malibu, CA 90265

GPS Coordinates: 34.03862° N, 118.68363° W

Did You Know? Malibu potteries only produced ceramic tiles for a small amount of time, but the tiles had a significant impact due to their vibrant colors.

Manhattan Beach

Manhattan Beach is the main beach in the town of the same name. The beach stretches for two miles and provides fantastic opportunities for surfing, swimming, and enjoying time in the sand.

Manhattan Beach Pier is 928 feet long with access to Roundhouse Aquarium, which offers free admission. Inside, visitors can view starfish and more up close. You can also take advantage of a paved path called The Strand to catch a glimpse of local vegetation and gorgeous scenery.

During the summer, Manhattan Beach sponsors a professional beach volleyball tournament with over 100 nets dotted along the beach. In downtown, you can visit art galleries, more than 150 retailers, and restaurants with award-winning chefs. In fact, Manhattan Beach is known as the "Pearl of the South Bay" for its amazing amenities.

Best Time to Visit: Manhattan Beach is open 24 hours.

Pass/Permit/Fees: Entry to Manhattan Beach is free. Parking costs depend on the lot.

Physical Address:
Manhattan Beach
4499–4401 The Strand
Manhattan Beach, CA 90266

GPS Coordinates: 34050° N, 118.42610° W

Did You Know? Roundhouse Aquarium was the location of the surf shop where Keanu Reeves purchased his surfboard in *Point Break*.

Redondo Beach

Redondo Beach is known as the birthplace of surfing for this area. In the early 1900s, George Freeth introduced the sport by surfing the local waves. Today, many surfers still flock to Redondo Beach for its relaxed vibe.

If you're not a surfer, the one and a half miles of shoreline surrounding Redondo Beach offer plenty of chances to shop along Riviera Village. This space is home to galleries, a farmer's market, specialty boutiques, and more.

Redondo Beach has California's only horseshoe-shaped pier, and the boardwalk is home to restaurants, shops, and attractions. Seaside Lagoon is a great stop for families, offering swimming and sunbathing at the family-friendly saltwater facility. Seaside Lagoon is open from Memorial Day to Labor Day.

If visiting the area in May, make sure to stop by BeachLife Festival. This annual beach party feature three days of live music, wonderful food, and more.

Best Time to Visit: Redondo Beach and the pier are open 24 hours a day, but the shops have separate hours.

Pass/Permit/Fees: Redondo Beach is free to enjoy.

Physical Address:
Redondo Beach Pier
Fisherman's Wharf
Redondo Beach, CA 90277

GPS Coordinates: 33.84251° N, 118.39070° W

Did You Know? The world record for the longest surf ride is three hours and 55 minutes. Gary Saavedra accomplished this feat in 2011 by riding in the wake of a speedboat.

Venice Beach

Venice Beach is a great place to visit while enjoying Los Angeles. Known for its eclectic boardwalk and energetic vibe, no other beach in the area offers the same flair.

Visitors to Venice Beach can enjoy surfing, swimming, kayaking, paddleboarding, and more. There are also picnic areas, places for fishing, plenty of shopping opportunities, and the ability to relax in the sun and enjoy the day.

On the boardwalk, over two miles of vendors and performers greet guests each day. You can also visit The Venice Beach Recreation Center to play sports or enjoy bodybuilding tournaments.

Venice Beach welcomes up to 30,000 people a day. When planning a trip, make sure to wear comfortable shoes and plan to stay for a few hours to enjoy everything the beach and boardwalk have to offer. Consider arriving mid-morning, as the beach is known to have fog in the early hours. The afternoons tend to be less crowded during the summer or on the weekends.

Best Time to Visit: Venice Beach is open daily from 8:00 a.m. to 7:00 p.m.

Pass/Permit/Fees: Venice Beach is free to enjoy. Parking fees depend on the lot.

Physical Address:
Venice Beach Recreation Center
1800 Ocean Front Walk
Venice, CA 90291

GPS Coordinates: 33.98557° N, 118.47283° W

Did You Know? In the 1920s, John Ringling made Sarasota County the winter headquarters of the Ringling Bros. and Barnum & Bailey Circus.

Festivals & Annual Events

Los Angeles is home to many festivals and annual events. Check each event's website to learn more about dates, times, and ticket information for each event. Additionally, tips and tricks for first-time attendees are readily available on many websites to help you plan your trip.

Tournament of Roses Parade

The Tournament of Roses Parade is held annually in Pasadena as the prequel to the Rose Bowl game later that same day. The first parade was in 1890, but it wasn't until 1902 that the football game was added to offset the cost of the parade. In 2011, Honda began sponsoring it.

Visitors to this New Year's Day celebration will be entertained by marching bands, singers, floats, and more. Each year, a theme is provided for the participants to follow. Floats in the parade must include natural materials such as flowers, seeds, bark, and leaves.

When planning a trip to the Tournament of Roses Parade, you should arrive at your spot the day before in the late afternoon or early evening. One of the best places to view the parade is from the southern side of Colorado Boulevard. For additional chances to enjoy the floats, head to The Showcase of Floats after the parade.

Best Time to Visit: The Tournament of Roses Parade is held on New Year's Day unless New Year's Day falls on a Sunday.

Pass/Permit/Fees: There is no cost associated with attending the parade, but reserved seats, parking, and The Showcase of Floats have varying fees. Advance tickets are not available for The Showcase of Floats.

Physical Address:
Parade Start
Corner of Green Street and Orange Grove Boulevard
Pasadena, CA 91101

GPS Coordinates: 34.14525° N, 118.15928° W

Did You Know? The Tournament of Roses Parade was originally called The Battle of the Flowers.

San Fernando Valley
Food & Wine Festival

The San Fernando Valley Food & Wine Festival is a culinary adventure with gourmet foods and fabulous wines. The event is hosted by the Los Angeles Mission College with proceeds going to the scholarship fund.

The Food & Wine Festival highlights over 200 featured wines. Breweries and restaurants also participate to offer a unique take on wine pairings. Guests are given a wine glass at the entrance and invited to enjoy indoor and outdoor vendors. There is also an entertainment area to sit and experience the festivities.

Best Time to Visit: Confirm the exact date and time each year before you visit.

Pass/Permit/Fees: General admission costs $99, and VIP admission costs $125. Advance tickets are available at a discounted rate of $75.

Physical Address:
Los Angeles Mission College
13356 Eldridge Avenue
Sylmar, CA 91342

GPS Coordinates: 33.84251° N, 118.39070° W

Did You Know? There are well over 4,000 wineries in California.

Día de los Muertos Art Walk

The Día de los Muertos Art Walk is held each October on Olvera Street in Los Angeles. Olvera Street is one of the oldest streets in the city with 10 miles of cobblestone roads running through the heart of LA.

The Día de los Muertos Art Walk is a celebration of culture and art in remembrance of loved ones who've passed on. Día de los Muertos can be traced back 2,500–3,000 years to the Aztec festival dedicated to the goddess known as Mictēcacihuātl, "The Lady of the Dead." The festival occurred during the corn harvest on the ninth month of the Aztec calendar.

The art walk is free and showcases local artists through mixed media, jewelry, sculpting, clothing, and more. In addition to enjoying the art provided, visitors can try local food and beverages, as well as learn more about Mexican culture and the true meaning of Día de los Muertos.

Best Time to Visit: Día de los Muertos Art Walk occurs toward the end of October each year. Confirm the date and time online prior to your visit.

Pass/Permit/Fees: Día de los Muertos Art Walk is free to attend. Parking is located nearby for varying fees.

Physical Address:
Día de los Muertos Art Walk
Olvera Street
Los Angeles, CA 90012

GPS Coordinates: 34.05762° N, 118.23793° W

Did You Know? Sugar skulls are brightly decorated in a whimsical style as a reminder that life goes on and should be celebrated.

LA County Fair

The LA County Fair began in the fall of 1922 with 5 days of entertainment. Today, the fair spans 16 days and is one of the largest county fairs in the United States.

Look online to decide which days you want to attend. Entertainment includes live music, attractions, and competitions in various categories. To receive the best price for tickets, purchase them online. Visitors who wish to go on rides will have the option to purchase ride packages. More than 60 rides and 30 games are available in the carnival section of the fair.

Best Time to Visit: Although subject to annual changes, the LA County Fair usually runs during the month of May.

Pass/Permit/Fees: Ticket prices cost between $15 and $25 for adults and $10 and $12 for children. Season passes are $29 each. Parking costs $17 if booked online or $22 at the gate. Carnival tickets and other attractions are priced separately.

Physical Address:
Fairplex
1101 W. McKinley Avenue
Pomona, CA 91768

GPS Coordinates: 34.08112° N, 117.76656° W

Did You Know? The Topsfield Fair in Massachusetts, which started in 1818, is the oldest county fair.

LA Beer Fest

The LA Beer Fest is in its 15th year. The event features over 80 breweries and 200 different kinds of beer. In addition, the Beer Fest hosts some of the best food trucks and live entertainment around.

Visitors to the LA Beer Fest can choose from general or Connoisseur admission. Both provide unlimited samples from the breweries and access to food trucks and entertainment. For guests who want a little more, the Connoisseur package includes access to the VIP lounge with air-conditioned bathrooms, an event deck, a festival t-shirt, and access to more beer options.

The LA Beer Fest is only for guests ages 21 and up. Pets are not allowed at the festival. To make the most of the experience, arrive early, wear comfortable clothing and shoes, eat a good breakfast, and hydrate with water along the way.

Best Time to Visit: Specific dates and times are subject to annual changes. Current dates and times are available online.

Pass/Permit/Fees: Tickets are nonrefundable, but attendees are allowed to sell their tickets if they cannot attend.

Physical Address:
Los Angeles Center Studios
450 S. Bixel Street
Los Angeles, CA 90017

GPS Coordinates: 34.05543° N, 118.2605° W

Did You Know? Dating back to 5000 BCE, beer is the oldest beverage in the world.

Zoos & Animals

Los Angeles is home to amazing zoos and aquariums. Many attractions offer a day's worth of fun for all ages. In addition to the ones listed, you can also enjoy the Beverly Hills Children's Zoo as a unique take on a "zoo." Located on private property, the yard offers fun animal statues that can easily be seen from the sidewalk. The statues include a 14-foot giraffe.

You may also appreciate the Deep Blue Aquarium in Hollywood. This unusual store carries an eclectic array of aquatic animals such as soft corals and mushrooms.

Los Angeles Zoo

The Los Angeles Zoo sits on 133 acres and houses over 1,100 animals and 29 endangered species. Additionally, there are over 7,500 plants to see at the zoo.

Visiting the Lost Angeles Zoo is a must for any vacation to the area. This popular landmark is well worth the visit and provides a wonderful look into animal habitats and ecosystems. Guests should plan to spend at least three hours exploring the zoo.

It's a good idea to look at a map of the zoo before your trip to decide what your group wants to see first. Popular stops are the Children's Zoo, Muriel's Ranch, The LAIR, Rainforests of the Americas, and the Australia House.

Food and beverages are available for purchase, and water fountains are spread throughout the space. You're allowed to bring your own food as long as you avoid glass and straws.

Best Time to Visit: The Los Angeles Zoo is open daily from 10:00 a.m. to 5:00 p.m.

Pass/Permit/Fees: Tickets must be purchased online to reserve a specific date and time, but they're also available at the gate. Admission is $22 for adults, $19 for children ages 2 and up, and free for children under 2.

Physical Address:
Los Angeles Zoo
5333 Zoo Drive
Los Angeles, CA 90027

GPS Coordinates: 34.14850° N, 118.28407° W

Did You Know? The oldest zoo in operation is the Vienna Zoo in Austria. It first opened in 1752.

Cabrillo Marine Aquarium

Cabrillo Marine Aquarium provides a living history of the marine animals that live in Southern California. The museum highlights these species and the conservation efforts in place to ensure their continued safety. Guests visiting the Cabrillo Marine Aquarium should plan to spend anywhere from two to three hours touring the space.

While there, be sure to visit the coastal park just outside the aquarium for a look at marshlands, native plant gardens, Cabrillo Beach, and salt marshes. The coastal park is fully accessible via walkways. You can enjoy fishing, boating, swimming, or birdwatching while there.

Inside the Cabrillo Marine Aquarium, exhibits focus on a variety of ecosystems in addition to displaying local marine life. Don't forget to stop by the aquatic nursery while you're here.

Best Time to Visit: The Cabrillo Marine Aquarium is open Tuesday through Sunday from 12:00 p.m. to 5:00 p.m. The gift shop is open Tuesday through Sunday from 10:00 a.m. to 5:30 p.m.

Pass/Permit/Fees: Admission costs $7 for adults and $3 for children or seniors.

Physical Address:
Cabrillo Marine Aquarium
3720 Stephen M. White Drive
San Pedro, CA 90731

GPS Coordinates: 33.71118° N, 118.28527° W

Did You Know? The Georgia Aquarium is the largest in the United States, with over 150,000 creatures and specimens to see.

Aquarium of the Pacific

The Aquarium of the Pacific is located on Rainbow Harbor in Long Beach. The 5-acre property is home to more than 12,000 animals in various tanks ranging from 5,000 to 350,000 gallons.

Visitors to the Aquarium of the Pacific are invited to learn more about animals in the Pacific Ocean through various exhibits, including a walk-through aviary and an outdoor cave.

Families with children will love the hands-on exhibits and ease of navigation throughout the space. You can also enjoy the 45-minute narrated Harbor Cruise or the Whale Watch and Dolphin Cruise for an additional cost.

A visitor guide and map are available to download online to help determine what you'd like to see first. Be aware that the aquarium does not allow strollers, but backpacks are available free of charge. For dining, there is a cafeteria-style restaurant on site. You may also pack a meal to enjoy at the picnic tables in the outside plaza.

Best Time to Visit: The Aquarium of the Pacific is open every day from 9:00 a.m. to 6:00 p.m.

Pass/Permit/Fees: Admission costs $36.95 for adults, $33.95 for seniors, and $26.95 for children 3 and up. Children under three may visit for free.

Physical Address:
Aquarium of the Pacific
100 Aquarium Way
Long Beach, CA 90802

GPS Coordinates: 33.76103° N, 118.19763° W

Did You Know? In Osaka, Japan, outdated telephone booths have been turned into aquariums.

Wildlife Learning Center

The Wildlife Learning Center was founded in 2007 to provide a home for animals in need. Staff at the Wildlife Learning Center offer education in life sciences, conservation, and environmental issues while caring for over 100 displaced animals.

Visitors to the Wildlife Learning Center have the unique opportunity to spend time with various animals face to face. These up-close encounters are available with sloths, a red-tailed boa, a porcupine, an owl, and an armadillo. At most, five people can participate at a time. These encounters are an additional cost, starting at $40.

When visiting the Wildlife Learning Center, consider joining one of two tours that provide an in-depth look into the center and the animals that live there. The Adventure Tour is the most interactive, allowing you to interact with a sloth, a reptile, a porcupine, and a tortoise.

Best Time to Visit: The Wildlife Learning Center is open Monday through Friday from 10:00 a.m. to 5:00 p.m.

Pass/Permit/Fees: Admission costs $15 for adults and $13 for seniors, teachers, military personnel, and children 3 and up. Children under three may visit for free. Advanced reservations are recommended.

Physical Address:
Wildlife Learning Center
16027 Yarnell Street
Sylmar, CA 91342

GPS Coordinates: 34.32074° N, 118.48007° W

Did You Know? Although sloths typically spend the day hanging out in trees, they are incredibly good swimmers.

Heal the Bay Aquarium

Heal the Bay Aquarium is located on the Santa Monica Pier. The aquarium has over 100 local species and provides hands-on activities and daily educational programs for all ages. Heal the Bay Aquarium is a certified green business and has won the Sustainable Quality Award.

This educational aquarium that works closely with local schools and visitors to help them better understand conservation in South Coast waters. Visitors can expect to spend around an hour at this attraction. There are eleven permanent exhibits, ranging from touch tanks to a kelp forest to an exhibit that gives you a glimpse under the Santa Monica Pier. Don't forget to stop by and see what else the Santa Monica Pier offers after visiting Heal the Bay Aquarium.

Best Time to Visit: Heal the Bay Aquarium is open Wednesday through Sunday from 12:00 p.m. to 4:00 p.m.

Pass/Permit/Fees: Admission is $10 for adults and free for children under 12.

Physical Address:
Heal the Bay Aquarium
1600 Ocean Front Walk
Santa Monica, CA 90401

GPS Coordinates: 34.01043° N, 118.49611° W

Did You Know? Heal the Bay Aquarium is passionate about ensuring that Southern California's beaches are clean. They coordinate several beach cleanups a year.

Theaters & Theatres

With a deep history in movie magic, it's no surprise that Los Angeles offers a plethora of theaters. From the iconic Hollywood Pantages Theatre to a marionette theatre that has over 100 unique puppets, visitors will be entertained no matter which landmark they choose.

More than 200 professional theater companies call Los Angeles home, and that doesn't include the many comedy clubs that are dotted throughout the area.

Long-running Los Angeles theater companies were frequently started by actors looking for a platform. Most have compact settings with fewer than 100 seats, allowing theatergoers to watch elite performers up close and personal in classics, brand-new shows, and musicals.

Hollywood Pantages Theatre

The Hollywood Pantages Theatre was the last theatre to be built by Alexander Pantages. It opened in 1930. With its Art Deco style, the theatre hosted vaudeville acts for the first two years before transitioning to first-run movies after the Great Depression.

Now, the Hollywood Pantages Theatre offers Broadway shows nearly every night of the year. Season or individual tickets can be purchased online. For a complete list of events, visit the Hollywood Pantages Theatre website.

When visiting, you'll marvel at the glamourous décor. After slight renovations over the years, the theater's last renovation returned it to the days of 1930 with velvet drapes and gold accents. During the restoration, nearly 300 artisans worked to return the building to its former glory.

Guests can dine before or after the show at one of many nearby restaurants. However, food and beverages are not allowed in the theater.

Best Time to Visit: Visit the Hollywood Pantages Theatre website for showtimes.

Pass/Permit/Fees: Ticket prices vary depending on the show and seat selection. There is a seating chart online to assist with purchasing.

Physical Address:
Hollywood Pantages Theatre
6233 Hollywood Boulevard
Los Angeles, CA 90028

GPS Coordinates: 34.10215° N, 118.32580° W

Did You Know? The longest-running Broadway musical is *The Phantom of the Opera*. It officially opened in 1988 and is still playing at The Majestic.

The Orpheum Theatre

The Orpheum Theatre opened in 1926. The Marx Brothers, Judy Garland, and Jack Benny performed on the stage during its early years. Since then, The Orpheum Theatre has hosted rock concerts, movie premieres, and more. The theatre has been featured in ten television shows, eight movies, and eight music videos.

Visitors to the theater can be entertained by various acts on several nights of the week. A calendar of events, as well as a seating chart to assist with purchasing tickets, is available online. When visiting The Orpheum, guests will also notice the 1928 Might Wurlitzer organ that's still in use today.

Many artists prefer that still cameras, video cameras, and recording devices not be allowed during the performance. Additionally, no outside food or beverages are permitted.

Best Time to Visit: The Orpheum Theatre offers a wide range of shows. A complete list and showtimes are available online.

Pass/Permit/Fees: Ticket prices depend on seating and the event. Tickets should be purchased online, and all tickets picked up at Will Call require a photo ID and the card used for the purchase.

Physical Address:
The Orpheum Theatre
842 S. Broadway
Los Angeles, CA 90014

GPS Coordinates: 34.04297° N, 118.25544° W

Did You Know? *Death of a Salesman* is considered the most historic American play. It is followed closely by *A Streetcar Named Desire*.

El Capitan Theatre

El Capitan Theatre opened in 1926, presenting live theater by actors such as Clark Gable and Joan Fontaine. For almost a decade, it hosted over 120 live productions on its stage before it started running movies.

The 1941 movie *Citizen Kane* premiered there when Orson Wells couldn't find another theater to host. Now, the theater hosts the majority of Walt Disney Studio's film productions.

Visitors can enjoy a variety of movies, from new to classics, in the renovated theater. After changing owners a few times, the most recent renovation was completed in 1991 prior to the premiere of *The Rocketeer*. The renovation captured the look of the original 1926 theater with ornate plasterwork and long, sweeping drapery.

For safety and security, all bags are subject to a search. Guests who leave the theater and return will be subject to an additional security check.

Best Time to Visit: Showtimes can be found online.

Pass/Permit/Fees: Pricing depends on the show and seat selection.

Physical Address:
El Capitan Theatre
6838 Hollywood Boulevard
Los Angeles, CA 90028

GPS Coordinates: 34.10156° N, 118.33995° W

Did You Know? Beginning with the 1937 movie *Snow White and the Seven Dwarves*, Disney has produced 61 feature films as of November 2022.

Bob Baker Marionette Theatre

The Bob Baker Marionette Theatre was founded in 1963 and is the oldest children's theater in Los Angeles. It has entertained over one million children with original shows and brilliant characters to this date. Not only does the staff at Bob Baker Marionette Theatre craft wonderful stories, but they also make their props and marionettes on site.

Visitors can enjoy one of several shows playing at the Bob Baker Marionette Theatre. The typical show lasts about an hour and has an average of 100 unique puppets. Seating is on the floor or in chairs. For the best chance of interacting with the puppets, the floor is the best option.

Puppet shows target all ages and display amazing creativity, craftsmanship, and imagination. The Bob Baker Marionette Theatre has over 2,000 puppets, some dating back to the 1940s. Watch the virtual tour on their website to get an inside look at the Bob Baker Marionette Theatre.

Best Time to Visit: Showtimes are listed online.

Pass/Permit/Fees: Tickets are typically $25.

Physical Address:
Bob Barker Marionette Theater
4949 York Boulevard
Los Angeles, CA 90042

GPS Coordinates: 34.12195° N, 118.20719° W

Did You Know? The first puppet on television was in 1930 during a showing of the London Marionette Theatre.

Pasadena Playhouse

The Pasadena Playhouse is a 686-seat auditorium in Pasadena that provides cultural and artistic entertainment through a wide variety of events. Once a small community playhouse, it now hosts multiple theatrical events yearly to sold-out crowds.

When visiting the Pasadena Playhouse, consult the website to see available shows. Be mindful that children under five will not be admitted. It is also important to arrive on time, as late arrivals will need to wait until the first break to be seated.

The theater is smaller in size, which provides an intimate setting. Due to the size, shows are viewed easily from all the seats. The venue offers a vintage experience that is welcomed and refreshing.

Food and beverages are not permitted in the theater, but there are several nearby restaurants to visit before or after the show. Tours are available for individuals and groups by calling or emailing.

Best Time to Visit: The Pasadena Playhouse offers a variety of shows. Check online to see the calendar of events.

Pass/Permit/Fees: Ticket prices typically start at $39 and vary depending on seating.

Physical Address:
Pasadena Playhouse
39 S. El Molino Avenue
Pasadena, CA 91101

GPS Coordinates: 34.14528° N, 118.13741° W

Did You Know? The longest running play in history is *The Mousetrap* by Agatha Christie. The play opened in 1952 and can still be seen at The Ambassador Theatre in London.

Mark Taper Forum

The Mark Taper Forum at the Los Angeles Music Center seats 739 guests and opened in 1967. The theater has an extensive production list, including five Tony Awards and several Ovation Awards. Additionally, the theater has hosted several world premieres such as *Jelly's Last Jam* and Neil Simon's *I Ought to Be in Pictures*. The Mark Taper Forum is a circular building with semi-circle seating that surrounds three sides of the stage. The design provides unique views of the stage and gives off an amphitheater vibe.

Tours of the Los Angeles Music Center are offered through guided and non-guided options. The Music Center Symphonian Tours are guided and provide in-depth looks at all four theaters located in the center, including the Mark Taper Forum.

When visiting, be mindful that cameras are not permitted. The theater has no dress code, although shirts and shoes are required. Food and beverage options are available in the lobby but are not allowed inside the theater itself.

Best Time to Visit: Consult the Mark Taper Forum calendar to see a list of events.

Pass/Permit/Fees: The cost depends on the event and seating. Parking is available in garages and by a valet. The cost varies depending on the garage.

Physical Address:
Mark Taper Forum
135 N. Grand Avenue
Los Angeles, CA 90012

GPS Coordinates: 34.05815° N, 118.24756° W

Did You Know? The Mark Taper Forum includes a thrust stage, a type of stage that extends into the audience.

Ahmanson Theatre

The Ahmanson Theatre is one of four main theatres in the Los Angeles Music Center. The theater's first event was held in 1967 in association with the Los Angeles Civic Light Opera Association. Since that time, the theater has hosted a variety of world premieres, as well as original productions. Over the years, it has won several Ovation Awards.

The theater offers an immersive experience with 2,109 seats. The design focuses on optimum viewing for musical comedy and theatrical productions with three levels of seating. Guests of the Ahmanson Theatre can enjoy food and beverage from one of many dining options, including food trucks from Tuesday through Thursday. Other options run from light choices to more formal seating. Food and drinks are not allowed in the theater.

Cameras are not permitted during productions. You should plan to arrive 10–15 minutes early to ensure you're in your seats prior to the start of the show.

Best Time to Visit: Consult the Los Angeles Music Center website to see showtimes and dates.

Pass/Permit/Fees: Parking is available in a nearby garage, as well as through the valet. The costs for productions and parking vary.

Physical Address:
Ahmanson Theatre
135 N. Grand Avenue
Los Angeles, CA 90012

GPS Coordinates: 34.05817° N, 118.24752° W

Did You Know? The Ahmanson Theatre has the largest theatrical season-ticket subscription base on the West Coast.

The Laugh Factory

The Laugh Factory is the perfect place to visit for engaging entertainment. Several locations exist, including the one in Los Angeles, which opened in 1979. Today, The Laugh Factory is one of the most renowned comedy clubs in the world. Shows are offered multiple times per week and feature famous comedians such as Dane Cook and Alonzo Bodden, as well as fresh faces in the comedy world.

There is no dress code, but guests must be 21 for entry or 18 with someone who is 21. Shows typically last an average of 70 minutes. You should plan to arrive at least 45 minutes before the start of the show. Seating is based on first arrivals.

No outside drinks or food are permitted in The Laugh Factory. Inside, there is a two-item minimum, meaning that each guest must purchase two items when making selections from the food and drink menu.

Best Time to Visit: Consult the website for showtimes and dates.

Pass/Permit/Fees: Ticket prices vary depending on the event. Parking costs are determined by location.

Physical Address:
The Laugh Factory
8001 Sunset Boulevard
Los Angeles, CA 90046

GPS Coordinates: 34.09842° N, 118.36453° W

Did You Know? Vaudeville artist Charlie Case is credited with the first stand-up comedy show.

Zombie Joe's
Underground Theatre

Zombie Joe's Underground Theatre opened in 1992 in a small industrial garage. Since then, the location has changed, but the mission of delivering cutting-edge, progressive theater remains.

Zombie Joe's calendar of events typically offers 40 shows per year, including an Urban Death Tour of Terror and an annual 50-Hour Drive-By Festival of short plays.

Visitors should note that most shows require guests to be at least 17 unless the event is labeled as family-friendly. Several restaurants are near the venue to visit before or after the show. No food or drink is permitted in the theater. Shows are not for the faint at heart and offer a unique twist on typical theatrical productions.

Best Time to Visit: Visit the website to see the times and dates of shows.

Pass/Permit/Fees: Parking is free nearby. The cost of admission is dependent on the show. Tickets are less expensive when purchased online in advance.

Physical Address:
Zombie Joe's Underground Theatre
4850 Lankershim Boulevard
Los Angeles, CA 91601

GPS Coordinates: 34.15935° N, 118.37089° W

Did You Know? Live theater dates back to the beginning of the fifth century in Athens.

Greek Theatre

The Greek Theatre in Los Angeles is an amphitheater in Griffith Park. The first performance occurred in 1931. For the first several years, the amphitheater was seldom used for its intended purpose since it was temporarily converted into barracks during World War II.

Now, the theater is regularly used for concerts, stage shows, and more. For eight years in a row, it won the Best Small Outdoor Venue award, offering a unique outdoor theater experience with nearly 6,000 seats.

When traveling with children, know that strollers are prohibited in the seating areas. They can be checked in at guest services. The artists determine whether cameras are allowed. Additionally, outside food and beverages are not permitted other than one bottle of factory-sealed water per guest. Dining options are available on site.

Best Time to Visit: Check the Greek Theatre website for event times and dates. All shows are rain or shine.

Pass/Permit/Fees: Parking is located in nearby lots and garages. The cost of parking and tickets varies based on selections. The Greek Theatre does not accept cash.

Physical Address:
The Greek Theatre
2700 N. Vermont Avenue
Los Angeles, CA 90027

GPS Coordinates: 34.11970° N, 118.29630° W

Did You Know? One of the most unusual theatres in the world is *The Seebuhne* floating theater in Austria.

Matrix Theatre

The Matrix Theatre in Los Angeles opened in 1977. It has won several Ovation Awards since opening. The Matrix Theatre has an old-school vibe with wooden-backed and cushioned chairs. Seating is graduated to provide optimal viewing for everyone.

Visitors can purchase tickets online or at the door. Tickets are nonrefundable but can be transferred to another performance. Please be aware that not all shows allow late seating. Be sure to arrive at least 15 minutes before the start of the show. Late arrivals that cannot be seated during the break will be offered the chance to attend a later production.

Pre- and post-theater dining for the Matrix Theatre can be found in nearby restaurants. No food or beverages are permitted in the theater.

Best Time to Visit: Showtimes and dates are available on the Matrix Theatre's website.

Pass/Permit/Fees: Parking is available nearby. Both show tickets and parking costs vary by selection.

Physical Address:
Matrix Theatre
7657 Melrose Avenue
Los Angeles, CA 90046

GPS Coordinates: 34.08401° N, 118.35665° W

Did You Know? There is an old superstition of no whistling on stage dates that back to the days when theaters hired sailors as stagehands and riggers. Cues were called using whistling commands, and any random whistling might have resulted in an accident.

El Portal Theatre

El Portal Theatre is located in North Hollywood. The theater is home to a variety of live performances several times a year. From comedy to musicals to concerts, there is something for everyone at El Portal Theatre.

Tickets are available online or at the door. The box office is available in person on show days or by phone. Tickets are nonrefundable and can't can be exchanged between people. If issues arise with ticketing, contact the box office immediately for assistance.

Visitors can enjoy nearby dining before or after their show. Snacks and drinks are also available on site for most shows. Please be aware that only cash is accepted at the concession stand. Additionally, cameras and audio or video are prohibited in the theater.

Plan to arrive at least 15 minutes before the show to find seats and purchase snacks. Late arrivals will be seated at the house manager's discretion. For some performances, last seating is not allowed.

Best Time to Visit: Check online for show dates and times.

Pass/Permit/Fees: Parking is available nearby. The cost of events and parking varies by selection.

Physical Address:
El Portal Theatre
5269 Lankershim Boulevard
North Hollywood, CA 91601

GPS Coordinates: 34.16709° N, 118.37601° W

Did You Know? The El Portal Theatre's main stage was renamed in 2017 to honor the sudden passing of Debbie Reynolds, who performed on stage 46 times between 2004 and 2014.

Other Attractions

When visiting Los Angeles, it is easy to find something to do each day. Take the time to map out a schedule to get the most out of your vacation. If opting for a guided tour, look for ones that offer stops at places your group is interested in visiting. Also, pay attention to discounted options to get the best prices. Many attractions require that tickets be purchased online.

Don't forget to check websites to confirm opening and closing information or find out more about dining options. The number of things to do in Los Angeles is staggering. Consider looking at online reviews to find the most popular places or see when those places might be less crowded.

Warner Brothers Studio

A visit to Warner Brothers Studio is an experience that should be included in any Los Angeles trip. The Warner Brothers began producing movies in 1927 with the release of *The Jazz Singer*.

There is a wide variety of tours to choose from, including the Studio Tour, the Classic Tour, and a Deluxe Tour. All tours can be previewed online to make the best choice for your group. Most tours offer an unguided and guided aspect. An average tour lasts three hours.

Walk-up tickets are limited. Since the studio is a working environment, not all areas will be available for every tour. In addition, parts of the studio do not permit photography. Be sure to arrive at least 30 minutes before your scheduled tour time. This allows for checking in, parking, and the mandatory security check.

Best Time to Visit: Warner Brothers Studio is open for tours every day from 8:30 a.m. to 3:30 p.m. except for June 13 and 14.

Pass/Permit/Fees: Ticket prices vary depending on the tour. Parking is available underground at the tour center for $15.

Physical Address:
Warner Bros. Studio Tour Hollywood
3400 Warner Boulevard
Burbank, CA 91505

GPS Coordinates: 34.15180° N, 118.33576° W

Did You Know? The Warner Brothers were a sibling group of four who took a chance that the American public would fall in love with the addition of speech and sound to movies.

WACKO/Soap Plant

The WACKO/Soap Plant combination shop is one of the most unique places to visit in Los Angeles. The WACKO/Soap Plant opened in 1971 and continues to sell soaps and lotions to this day. In addition, the shop features a unique inventory from collectibles to tarot cards to funky socks and more.

The outside of the store is just as eclectic and vibrant as the inside, offering an assortment of items that can't be found anywhere else. Over time, the store has grown to absorb the two neighboring businesses to make one large space.

Visitors will enjoy roaming through the aisles, finding fun gifts to purchase as souvenirs of their time in Los Angeles. Plan to spend at least an hour inside. With so many things on the shelves, it will be hard to see it all.

Best Time to Visit: WACKO/Soap Plant is open Monday through Saturday from 11:00 a.m. to 7:00 p.m. and Sunday from 11:00 a.m. to 6:00 p.m.

Pass/Permit/Fees: Enjoying WACKO/Soap Plant is free. Parking is located nearby with varying costs.

Physical Address:
WACKO/Soap Plant
4633 Hollywood Boulevard
Los Angeles, CA 90027

GPS Coordinates: 34.10047° N, 118.29005° W

Did You Know? The earliest soap was made around 2800 BCE by the Babylonians. Liquid soap, which many American use today, was invented in 1865.

Two Bit Circus

Two Bit Circus offers everything from old-school carnival games to modern escape rooms. Visitors can enjoy taking their chance in the Two Bit Circus Story Rooms, dubbed the "Escape Room of the Future." The rooms require interaction and problem-solving skills in themed environments.

The Arena is also an option when visiting Two Bit Circus. This space is the best of the best when it comes to virtual-reality gaming. If classics are more your style, hop on over to the Arcade, where classic cabinet games are all the rage. Carnival games like Skee-Ball are available in the Midway.

Walk-ins are allowed, but it's best to book packages online to receive additional bonuses and ensure availability. Food and beverages are offered on site as well.

Best Time to Visit: Two Bit Circus is open Thursday from 6:00 p.m. to 11:00 p.m., Friday and Saturday from 4:00 p.m. to 1:00 p.m., and Sunday from 1:00 p.m. to 8:00 p.m.

Pass/Permit/Fees: Parking structures and street parking are available nearby. The price for packages varies by selection. Two Bit Circus does not accept cash. Be mindful that each guest must purchase a package whether or not they plan to play.

Physical Address:
Two Bit Circus
634 Mateo Street
Los Angeles, CA 90021

GPS Coordinates: 34.03723° N, 118.23200° W

Did You Know? The oldest carnival game is the Milk Bottle Knockdown.

The Last Bookstore

The Last Bookstore is one of the largest used bookstores in California. At 22,000 square feet, The Last Bookstore a plethora of comics, records, books, and more.

Besides browsing through a fantastic assortment of media, visitors can enjoy the book tunnel, finding hidden nooks with unique items, and viewing a mammoth head that's on display. The Last Bookstore opened in 2005 and is housed in a former bank building, complete with the old vault.

When visiting The Last Bookstore, be sure to check out Gather Yarn Shop and Dave Lovejoy Art, both of which are located on the mezzanine level. There is also a rare book annex tucked amongst the 225,000 new and used books on display. Guests should plan to spend at least an hour enjoying everything The Last Bookstore has to offer.

Best Time to Visit: The Last Bookstore is open every day from 11:00 a.m. to 8:00 p.m.

Pass/Permit/Fees: Paid parking is located nearby. The Last Bookstore does not charge an entry fee.

Physical Address:
The Last Bookstore
453 South Spring Street, ground floor
Los Angeles, CA 90013

GPS Coordinates: 34.04789° N, 118.24983° W

Did You Know? The Andover Bookstore, founded in 1809, is the oldest independent bookstore in the United States.

Time Travel Mart

Time Travel Mart is located in Echo Park. It's a perfect place to stop for a break from the sun while enjoying the many activities available in the area.

Time Travel Mart opened in 2008 and offers a variety of unique treasures. As a convenience store with gadgets from the past, present, and future, it can feel like shopping in a time loop. The Time Travel Market is also home to the publishing company Barnacle & Barnacle Publishers, specializing in original student-authored books.

Visitors will enjoy walking through the aisles of novelty items, which includes books, apparel, writing accessories, art, and gifts. Food and beverages are not permitted in the space to minimize damage to the merchandise.

While at The Time Travel Mart, be sure to ask about the 826LA nonprofit that is run by the store. The nonprofit provides free educational services to students, focusing on creative and expository writing skills.

Best Time to Visit: Time Travel Mart is open every day from 12:00 p.m. to 6:00 p.m.

Pass/Permit/Fees: Paid parking is available on the street and in nearby garages.

Physical Address:
Time Travel Mart
1714 Sunset Boulevard
Los Angeles, CA 90026

GPS Coordinates: 34.07752° N, 118.25902° W

Did You Know? Science has a number of different ways to differentiate time, including astronomical and atomic time.

Hollywood Walk of Fame

The Hollywood Walk of Fame is a historic landmark encompassing 15 blocks of Hollywood Boulevard. To date, there are over 2,700 stars on the Walk of Fame. These stars celebrate actors, directors, musicians, and even fictional characters.

Visitors to the Hollywood Walk of Fame can take pictures with some of their favorite stars' names while reminiscing about the shows and movies they enjoyed the most. The full experience will take around an hour. Mornings are best for a quieter visit, or you can book a guided tour to learn more about the individuals featured here.

Anyone can nominate someone for a star on the Hollywood Walk of Fame. Candidates are approved through a voting process once a year. On average, 30 people are chosen each year. To find out who has a star on the Walk of Fame or learn about upcoming ceremonies, visit the Hollywood Walk of Fame website.

Best Time to Visit: The Hollywood Walk of Fame is open 24 hours.

Pass/Permit/Fees: Plan to park in one of the nearby garages or lots to enjoy other activities in the area.

Physical Address:
Hollywood Walk of Fame
Hollywood Boulevard, Vine Street
Los Angeles, CA 90028

GPS Coordinates: 34.10225° N, 118.32690° W

Did You Know? Gene Autry is the only person to be awarded five stars on the Hollywood Walk of Fame.

Universal Studios Hollywood

Universal Studios Hollywood is a film studio and amusement park that opened to the public in 1915. The entire family can enjoy a day at Universal Studios Hollywood, whether on the rides or learning more about the studio during a tour.

Universal Studios Hollywood is made up of themed areas that celebrate some of the most iconic movies and television shows in history. From Minion Land to The Wizarding World of Harry Potter, the magic and adventure last all day.

You can also take a studio tour that puts you front and center in the action. With 13 blocks spread over a 400-acre historic lot, the tour provides a wonderful look at the history of Universal Studios from backstage. The 60-minute tour is now included with park admission.

Visitors planning to enjoy The Wizarding World of Harry Potter should head there first, as lines get long quickly. Additionally, plan on arriving at the park at least 30 minutes before it opens.

Best Time to Visit: Park hours vary throughout the year. For the most up-to-date information, check online.

Pass/Permit/Fees: Ticket prices vary depending on the package selected. Purchasing advance tickets and Universal Express Passes is highly recommended.

Physical Address:
Universal Studios Hollywood
100 Universal City Plaza
Universal City, CA 91608

GPS Coordinates: 34.13832° N, 118.35340° W

Did You Know? E.T. Adventure is the last remaining original ride in the park.

Hollywood Sign

Construction for the Hollywood sign started in 1923. One hundred years later, it is one of the most iconic landmarks in the world. Some of the best views of the Hollywood Sign can be seen on the corner of Hollywood Boulevard and Highland. The sign is also clearly visible from the Hollywood Walk of Fame. Another wonderful spot to catch a glimpse of the sign is at Griffith Observatory. Entrance to the Observatory is free, offering a bird's eye view.

Visitors who want a different view of the Hollywood Sign can take one of several trails. The trails are open from sunrise to sunset every day of the year. The easiest trail is the Mount Hollywood Trail, which starts in Griffith Park. The distance is just over five miles, and it takes an average of two and a half hours to complete. Be mindful that there is little shade on this trail, so be sure to bring water.

Another trail to consider is the Brush Canyon Trail. This trail also starts in Griffith Park, and it takes an average of three hours to complete the six-mile trek. This is a slightly more challenging trail that's a favorite for hikers and runners.

Best Time to Visit: Since the sign does not have lighting, plan to arrive earlier rather than later.

Pass/Permit/Fees: There is no charge to view the sign. Parking costs are dependent on location.

Physical Address:
Hollywood Sign Viewpoint
3114 Canyon Lake Drive
Los Angeles, CA 90068

GPS Coordinates: 34.12881° N, 118.32614° W

Did You Know? The Hollywood Sign was created as a real estate advertisement in 1923.

Grand Central Market

Grand Central Market is the largest and oldest public market in Los Angeles. It opened in 1917 and was collectively ranked as one of America's Best New Restaurants in 2014 for all the restaurants located within the market.

Grand Central Market is spread out over 30,000 square feet and 40 stalls. The mix of food and retail shopping provides an eclectic experience for the senses.

Beyond shopping, Grand Central Market hosts numerous events each year, including a weekly bazaar that welcomes new merchants every Friday, Saturday, and Sunday starting at 11:00 a.m. Live music is also a frequent event at Grand Central Market.

Best Time to Visit: As a whole, Grand Central Market is open every day from 8:00 a.m. to 9:00 p.m. Each vendor has their own hours, so be mindful when shopping that not all vendors are open at the same time.

Pass/Permit/Fees: Grand Central Market has on-site parking next to the market. Parking rates are $4 for the first 90 minutes. Each additional 15 minutes is $2. There is a daily maximum of $25.

Physical Address:
Grand Central Market
317 S. Broadway
Los Angeles, CA 90013

GPS Coordinates: 34.05148° N, 118.24922° W

Did You Know? The world's largest public market, the Chatuchak Weekend Market, is in Bangkok, Thailand.

The Grove

The Grove is an outdoor shopping experience adjacent to Originals Farmers Market in Los Angeles. An electric-powered streetcar runs between both sites, connecting shoppers to a varied shopping experience.

The Grove is a wonderful place to spend the day shopping in luxury. Each building was painstakingly crafted to exude brilliance and glamour. A layout and description of included stores can be found online. In addition, pop-up shops offer a revolving range of products for shoppers to enjoy. World-class dining is also available in the space, making it easy to come early and spend the whole day.

When visiting with family, take advantage of amenities like the Family Room, which includes changing tables, children's play areas, nursing rooms, and more. In addition, every Thursday from 10:00 a.m. and 11:00 features storytelling, puppets, and live music.

Best Time to Visit: The Grove is open Monday through Thursday from 10:00 a.m. to 9:00 p.m., Friday and Saturday from 10:00 a.m. to 10:00 p.m., and Sunday from 11:00 a.m. to 8:00 p.m.

Pass/Permit/Fees: Valet parking is available from 10:00 a.m. to 10:00 p.m. daily. Rates are available starting at $12 for the first hour. The daily maximum is $30 for 5 hours.

Physical Address:
The Grove
189 The Grove Drive
Los Angeles, CA 90036

GPS Coordinates: 34.07209° N, 118.35753° W

Did You Know? At over 12 million square feet, Dubai Mall is the largest mall in the world.

The Americana at Brand

The Americana at Brand is a high-class outdoor shopping experience. Offering a variety of world-renowned restaurants and retail establishments, The Americana at Brand takes retail therapy to the next level.

Beyond a wonderful shopping experience, The Americana at Brand offers multiple family-friendly events, including live entertainment, storytelling, puppet shows, a piano bar at Bourbon Steak Los Angeles, and a running club at Lululemon. Check the website for any events that are happening during your visit.

Highlights include a ride on the trolley, the fountain at the center of The Green, and daily specials from some of the best brands around. Visitors with children will enjoy the Family Room, which features play areas and changing tables when the younger ones need a break from shopping.

Best Time to Visit: The Americana at Brand is open Monday through Thursday from 10:00 a.m. to 9:00 p.m., Friday and Saturday from 10:00 a.m. to 10:00 p.m., and Sunday from 11:00 a.m. to 8:00 p.m.

Pass/Permit/Fees: Valet and self-parking are available. The cost depends on the amount of time spent at The Americana. The daily maximum is $24 for self-parking and $30 for valet.

Physical Address:
The Americana at Brand
889 Americana Way
Glendale, CA 91210

GPS Coordinates: 34.14503° N, 118.25647° W

Did You Know? The Mall of America, located in Bloomington, MN, is the largest shopping center in the United States.

The Original Farmers Market

The Original Farmers Market opened in 1934. Today, it has over 100 food and retail vendors. Located next to The Grove, there is an electric streetcar that runs in between the two.

A map with store names is available online to help visitors plan their trip. Foodies can even take advantage of the Farmers Market Food and History Tour offered by Melting Pot Food Tours Original to learn about the market and sample food from different vendors. The tour is $50 and lasts for 2.5 hours with 10 stops. Tours are every Wednesday, Friday, and Saturday from 9:30 a.m. to 12:00 p.m.

Shopping at The Original Farmers Market will allow you to try things you may not have seen before. Take advantage of samples, and keep an open mind.

Best Time to Visit: The Original Farmers Market is open Monday through Friday from 9:00 a.m. to 9:00 p.m., Saturday from 9:00 a.m. to 8:00 p.m., and Sunday from 9:00 a.m. to 7:00 p.m.

Pass/Permit/Fees: The Original Farmers Market has two convenient lots. Visitors can get 90 minutes of free validation with a purchase or 2-hour validation from select vendors. Fees are $3.50 for the first 15 minutes beyond the 90-minute validation period and an additional $1.50 for each 15 minutes after that. The maximum price per day is $32.

Physical Address:
The Original Farmers Market
6333 W. 3rd Street
Los Angeles, CA 90036

GPS Coordinates: 34.07220° N, 118.36036° W

Did You Know? The Lancaster Central Market in Lancaster, PA, is the oldest farmers market in the nation. The market opened in 1730.

Rodeo Drive

Rodeo Drive is one of the most well-known streets in the nation. The two-mile stretch of road in Beverly Hills has been featured in many movies and television shows.

Rodeo Drive is home to more than 100 shops that are often household names. Visitors can also enjoy world-class dining from Michelin-rated chefs. A walk through Rodeo Drive offers the opportunity to enjoy palm trees, architectural marvels, and a sense of wonderment. Guests can expect to spend one to two hours just enjoying the exterior of the buildings or more if shopping is involved.

When visiting Rodeo Drive, take time to window shop. The impressive displays will delight your senses. Carolers can be heard singing on the streets during the holidays.

Beyond shopping, Rodeo Drive is also home to art galleries. Take a look at Galerie Michael, which has four decades of art on display, or stop by the Mouche Gallery for contemporary art.

Best Time to Visit: Most stores on Rodeo Drive are open Monday through Saturday from 10:00 a.m. to 6:00 p.m. and Sunday from 12:00 p.m. to 5:00 p.m.

Pass/Permit/Fees: Several parking options exist around Rodeo Drive. The cost depends on the lot. Within the city of Beverly Hills, spots with red diamond indicate free parking for two hours.

Physical Address:
Rodeo Drive
Los Angeles, CA 90210

GPS Coordinates: 34.06797° N, 118.40163° W

Did You Know? In *Pretty Woman*, Richard Gere is actually playing the piano. Not only that, but he composed the piece himself.

Hollywood Forever Cemetery

The Hollywood Forever Cemetery is the final resting place for more stars than anywhere else in the world. Founded in 1899, it's also Hollywood's only cemetery.

Visitors are allowed to walk the grounds, viewing the final resting places of stars like Judy Garland, Mickey Rooney, Chris Cornell, and more. Tours can be scheduled online if you'd like to get an in-depth look into the cemetery's history.

Best Time to Visit: Hollywood Forever Cemetery is open Monday through Friday from 8:30 a.m. to 5:00 p.m. and weekends from 8:30 a.m. to 4:30 p.m.

Pass/Permit/Fees: Visiting the cemetery is free. The Cemetery of the Stars Tour lasts approximately 2.5 hours and costs $25 per person. Night Tours are also available throughout the year for $50 per person. Parking is available at the funeral home or in nearby lots.

Physical Address:
Hollywood Forever Cemetery
6000 Santa Monica Boulevard
Los Angeles, CA 90038

GPS Coordinates: 34.08905° N, 118.31905° W

Did You Know? Florence Lawrence was the first star buried in the Hollywood Forever Cemetery in 1886.

Madame Tussauds Hollywood

Madame Tussauds Hollywood opened in 2009, making it the fourth American site. The wax museum is home to 125 celebrity likenesses. Visitors to Madame Tussauds Hollywood can visit one of several zones, including Pop Icons and Country Western. There is also a special area dedicated to Marvel superheroes. While there, you can pretend you're interacting with superheroes or walking the red carpet with stars like Demi Lovato or Dwayne "The Rock" Johnson.

Be aware that outside food and drinks are prohibited, but there are concessions available inside. Madame Tussauds Hollywood is a self-guided experience lasting anywhere from 60 to 90 minutes. Guests should be 18 unless supervised by an adult.

Best Time to Visit: Madame Tussauds Hollywood is open Sunday through Thursday from 11:00 a.m. to 6:00 p.m. and Friday and Saturday from 10:00 a.m. to 8:00 p.m.

Pass/Permit/Fees: General admission is $32.99. Tickets can be purchased online. Some attractions, including Marvel Universe 4D, have an additional cost. Parking is available in the garage under Madame Tussauds or at the Hollywood and Highland Center.

Physical Address:
Madame Tussauds Hollywood
6933 Hollywood Boulevard
Los Angeles, CA 90028

GPS Coordinates: 34.10190° N, 118.34153° W

Did You Know? Each Madame Tussauds location has different figures on display.

Pink's Hot Dogs

Pink's Hot Dogs has been a landmark in Los Angeles since 1939. The iconic restaurant serves over 2,000 hot dogs per day. Pink's Hot Dogs have been mentioned in several movies, television shows, and books during its history.

Many celebrities have frequented Pink's Hot Dogs to enjoy hot dogs named after their show or themselves. Menu options include The Big Bang Theory, Mulholland Drive Dog, and The Ozzy Spice Dog, to name a few. The menu consists of 40 different types of hot dogs and 12 varieties of hamburgers.

Pink's Hot Dogs are different from any other hot dog due to the distinct snap when you bite them. Pink's Hot Dogs is family owned and now has 13 locations and a catering business. When visiting Pink's Hot Dogs, take time to look at the menu to find the right fit. Additionally, check out the dining room, which has over 200 pictures of celebrities with signed endorsements of their love for Pink's Hot Dogs.

Best Time to Visit: Pink's Hot Dogs is open Sunday through Thursday from 9:30 a.m. to 12:00 p.m. and Friday and Saturday from 9:30 a.m. to 2:00 a.m.

Pass/Permit/Fees: Parking is available at Pink's Hot Dogs and nearby lots. Fees are determined by the lot.

Physical Address:
Pink's Hot Dogs
709 N. La Brea Avenue
Los Angeles, CA 90038

GPS Coordinates: 34.08405° N, 118.34422° W

Did You Know? Fort Wayne's Hot Dog Stand in Coney Island is America's oldest hot dog stand.

Mulholland Drive

Mulholland Drive is home to several celebrities, and it's a popular destination for tourists. The road is 55 miles long and connects Hollywood Hills to Leo Carrillo State Beach in Malibu. However, driving the entire 55 miles is difficult as part of the road is not easily passable by car.

Visitors who want to see Mulholland Drive can drive up the Hollywood Hills from US-101 via Cahuenga Boulevard. The 20-mile drive will take about an hour, not including stops along the way. Guests can also opt to take the Mulholland Drive Scenic Overlook from US-101, covering less distance but still enjoying fantastic views.

When driving, be sure to stop to get the best views of the city. Overlook points include the Jerome C. Daniel Overlook, which gives visitors a look at the Hollywood sign and Griffith Observatory. From the Universal City Overlook, guests can see Hogwarts Castle and the San Fernando Valley below. If driving isn't an option, you can enjoy Mulholland Drive by guided tour. Several options are available for tours of the famous road.

Best Time to Visit: Visiting during the day is best to get the most out of the scenery.

Pass/Permit/Fees: Mulholland Drive is free to access. If you choose to take a guided tour, costs vary depending on your exact selection.

Physical Address:
Mulholland Scenic Overlook
8591 Mulholland Drive
Los Angeles, CA 90046

GPS Coordinates: 34.15840° N, 118.37134° W

Did You Know? The movie *Mulholland Drive* started as a television pilot.

Musso & Frank Grill

Musso & Frank Grill is located on Hollywood Boulevard. The restaurant opened in 1919 and was initially called Frank's Francois Café. In 1923, the restaurant was sold to Joseph Musso, who changed the name to Musso & Frank Grill. The restaurant changed hands again in 1927 when it was purchased by the Mosso family that still owns it today.

Visitors to Musso & Frank Grill will recognize it from movies and television shows such as *Ocean's Eleven, Mad Men, Bosch, Once Upon a Time in Hollywood*, and more. The establishment looks very similar to when it opened, providing guests with a feeling of timelessness.

The menu at Musso & Frank Grill offers classic steakhouse favorites like braised short ribs and filet mignon. Reservations are recommended and can be booked online.

Best Time to Visit: The Musso & Frank Grill is open Tuesday through Saturday from 5:00 p.m. to 11:00 p.m. and Sunday from 4:00 p.m. to 10:00 p.m.

Pass/Permit/Fees: There is on-site parking at Musso & Frank Grill, including valet parking. The cost of parking varies depending on the lot and services used.

Physical Address:
Musso & Frank Grill
6667 Hollywood Boulevard
Hollywood, CA 90028

GPS Coordinates: 34.10189° N, 118.33534° W

Did You Know? The world-famous Hollywood sign once said Hollywoodland.

Paramount Pictures Studio

Paramount Pictures is the longest-operating and only remaining major studio in Hollywood. The studio lot sits on 65 acres and has 30 stages. Visitors to Paramount Pictures Studio can view some of the most iconic sets in movie history.

Studio tours are typically available every day of the year except for major holidays. Tours depart every 15 to 30 minutes and can be booked online. Walk-ups are welcome, but due to high demand, reserving tickets online is the best way to ensure entry.

When traveling with children, please note that there is an age limit of 10 and over. Children under 18 must be accompanied by an adult. Still photography is allowed on the tour, but recording is prohibited. The tour lasts approximately two hours. You should plan to arrive 30 minutes before the start. During the tour, you can expect to see locations such as the Bronson Gate, a New York street backlot, and the prop warehouse during the tour.

Best Time to Visit: Paramount Pictures Studio tours run every day from 8:30 a.m. to 4:00 p.m.

Pass/Permit/Fees: Tickets cost $58. Parking is available at the visitor lot across from the studios. Parking is $22 unless visiting for a VIP tour.

Physical Address:
Paramount Pictures Studio Tour
5515 Melrose Avenue
Los Angeles, CA 90038

GPS Coordinates: 34.08394° N, 118.32089° W

Did You Know? The first Paramount Pictures production was a French silent film named *The Loves of Queen Elizabeth* in 1912.

La Brea Tar Pits and Museum

The La Brea Tar Pits and Museum is an active research site. The site has produced several fossils, including the remains of a saber-toothed cat, ground sloths, bison, and more. It is the world's only active Ice Age excavation site.

At the museum, guests can learn more about the La Brea Tar Pits and see fossil deposits and the pits up close. You should plan to spend one to two hours at the museum.

When arriving, be sure to pick up a Discovery Guide, which contains a map of the exhibits. Be mindful that the museum has attractions both inside and outside. There is also a 3D theater and a show called *Ice Age Encounters*. Favorite exhibits at the La Brea Tar Pits and Museum include the Fossil Lab and experiencing sticky asphalt.

Best Time to Visit: La Brea Tar Pits and Museum is open every day from 9:30 a.m. to 5:00 p.m.

Pass/Permit/Fees: Admission costs $15 for adults, $12 for students or seniors, and $7 for children. Special exhibits have an additional cost.

Physical Address:
La Brea Tar Pits and Museum
5801 Wilshire Boulevard
Los Angeles, CA 90036

GPS Coordinates: 34.06412° N, 118.35543° W

Did You Know? Since 1906, 1 million bones have been found in the La Brea Tar Pits, collectively representing over 231 species of vertebrates. Archeologists continue to discover new fossils to this day.

Disneyland

Disneyland opened in 1923. Visitors can spend anywhere from one day to a week or more enjoying the many attractions, including new rides added within the past few years.

When visiting Disneyland, note that there are two theme parks: the original Disneyland and Disneyland California Adventure Park. Both offer various things for people of all ages. Two of the most popular attractions are Star Wars: Galaxy's Edge in Disneyland and Avengers Campus in Adventure Park.

For the best experience, plan to stay at a Disneyland hotel. The attached hotels have a shuttle service to and from the parks as well as an option for early entry.

Best Time to Visit: Disneyland is open Thursday through Sunday and Tuesday from 8:00 a.m. to 12:00 a.m. It's also open Monday and Wednesday from 8:00 a.m. to 11:00 p.m.

Pass/Permit/Fees: A 1-day parking voucher is $30. Ticket costs for the parks vary on the package purchased. A standard ticket starts at $83 per day.

Physical Address:
Disneyland Park
1313 Disneyland Drive
Anaheim, CA 92802

GPS Coordinates: 33.82093° N, 117.91932° W

Did You Know? Download the Disneyland mobile app for up-to-date information on wait times, show listings, and more.

Sony Pictures Studios

Sony Pictures Studios was founded in 1912. Sony Pictures is the parent company of Columbia Pictures, TriStar Pictures, and Screen Gems. Many films and television shows have been filmed on set over the years, including *The Goldbergs*, *Shark Tank,* and *Wheel of Fortune.*

Visitors to Sony Pictures Studios can take the studio tour, which lasts about two hours. This guided walking tour gives guests a behind-the-scenes look at several iconic shows and films. Sound stages from *The Wizard of Oz, Men in Black, Jeopardy!*, and more are included.

Tours are available Monday through Friday. Reservations are required. When traveling with children, take note that children under the age of 12 are not permitted. There are several options for tours, such as a twilight tour on Thursday evenings and a three-hour VIP lunch tour that includes a three-course meal and a visit to the Sony Museum.

Best Time to Visit: Check the website for tour times.

Pass/Permit/Fees: Parking is free. Tours start at $50.

Physical Address:
Sony Pictures Studios
10202 Washington Boulevard
Culver City, CA 90232

GPS Coordinates: 34.01790° N, 118.40104° W

Did You Know? Sony Pictures's biggest franchises include Spider-Man, Men in Black, and James Bond.

Crypto.com Arena

The Crypto.com Arena, formerly known as the Staples Center, is the home of the Lakers and Clippers professional men's basketball teams, the Kings hockey team, and the Sparks women's basketball team.

Additionally, the Crypto.com Arena hosts many other events such as concerts throughout the year. Bags of any kind are not allowed. Small clutches or wallets that are smaller than 5 x 9 x 1 inches are permitted but subject to security checks.

Crypto.com Arena has a variety of dining options within the facility. Outside food and drinks are not allowed. Additionally, Cryto.com Arena is a smoke-free facility. Doors for all ticketed events will open one and a half hours prior to the start of the event.

Best Time to Visit: Check the calendar of events for dates and times.

Pass/Permit/Fees: Several lots are available for parking, including lots with EV charging stations. Parking costs and event prices are dependent on the lot and the event. Tickets must be purchased online in advance.

Physical Address:
Crypto.com Arena
1111 S. Figueroa Street
Los Angeles, CA 90015

GPS Coordinates: 34.04320° N, 118.26722° W

Did You Know? During the 1971–1972 NBA season, the Los Angeles Lakers set the record for the league's longest streak by winning 33 games in a row.

Six Flags Magic Mountain

Six Flags Magic Mountain opened in 1971 and now spans over 260 acres. With 20 roller coasters, Six Flags Magic Mountain holds the record for the most roller coasters in one park. You can download the official Six Flags Mobile app to plan your visit and plot routes between more than 100 rides.

Six Flags Magic Mountains also offers entertainment, shopping, dining, and more. When visiting, check ride restrictions ahead of time to know which rides are appropriate for children. Additionally, schedule your trip with peak times in mind. Holidays and school breaks tend to be more crowded.

Arrive at least a half hour before the park opens to find parking and get in line. It takes time to go through security, so be prepared.

Best Time to Visit: Six Flags Magic Mountain is open Thursday, Friday, and Sunday from 10:30 a.m. to 6:00 p.m., Saturday from 10:30 a.m. to 8:00 p.m., and Monday from 10:30 a.m. to 5:00 p.m.

Pass/Permit/Fees: Tickets start at $54.99 and do not include parking. Parking is $40 for a 1-day general parking pass.

Physical Address:
Six Flags Magic Mountain
26101 Magic Mountain Parkway
Valencia, CA 91355

GPS Coordinates: 34.42548° N, 118.59723° W

Did You Know? Gold Rusher, the park's first roller coaster, is the oldest ride at Six Flags Magic Mountain.

Hollywood City Tours

Hollywood City Tours is one of the best ways to enjoy the sights and sounds of Hollywood. Tour options range from two hours to seven hours, with loads of information and attractions in each.

The Original Hollywood Tour lasts for two hours and focuses on Hollywood, West Hollywood, and Beverly Hills. Guests ride in an open-air bus and are shown some of the hottest attractions in the area.

Tour hotspots include the Walk of Fame, Capitol Records, Laugh Factory, Sunset Strip, filming locations, and more. The tour also includes the homes of stars such as Madonna to Johnny Depp, among others.

The Grand LA Tour focuses on the same areas, plus stops at the Santa Monica Pier, the Original Farmers Market, Griffith Observatory, and the Walk of Fame. Both tours offer a wealth of information about each stop and attraction along the way.

Best Time to Visit: Hollywood City Tours run every day from 9:00 a.m. to 9:00 p.m.

Pass/Permit/Fees: Parking is available for $15. The Original Holiday Tour prices are $39 for adults and $29 for children under 10. The Grand LA Tour prices are $95 for adults and $75 for children under 10.

Physical Address:
Hollywood City Tours
6437 Sunset Boulevard
Los Angeles, CA 90028

GPS Coordinates: 34.09836° N, 118.33013° W

Did You Know? Muhamad Ali is the only person whose Hollywood Walk of Fame star is not on the ground.

Marvin Braude Bike Trail

The Marvin Braude Bike Trail, also known as the Beach Bike Path and Coastal Bike Trail, is a 22-mile paved path along Santa Monica Bay's shoreline. The ends of the trail are at Will Rogers State Beach and Via Riviera on one side and Paseo de la Playa on the other. The bike path is open to bicyclists, in-line skaters, and walkers. It is also wheelchair accessible.

While on the bike path, you can take in cliffside houses, the fun at Santa Monica Pier, the quirkiness of Venice Beach, miles of shoreline, and the sound of the ocean waves. Keep an eye on your progress by downloading a map.

Be sure to bring water for hydration and dress for the weather. The trail goes through several areas where you can stop to dine or shop.

Best Time to Visit: The Marvin Braude Bike Trail is open year round from sunup to sundown.

Pass/Permit/Fees: Parking is available all along the trail. The cost is dependent on the lot. The trail itself is free to use.

Physical Address:
Marvin Braude Bike Trail (Lower Pier Lots)
1125–1199 N. The Strand
Manhattan Beach, CA 90266

GPS Coordinates: 33.88496° N, 118.41213° W

Did You Know? The East Coast Greenway is a substantial network of urban trails that runs between Key West, Florida; and Calais, Maine; through 15 states and 450 cities and towns. It is the longest single walking and biking track in the country.

Hike in Eaton Canyon

Eaton Canyon Trail is a 4.4-mile out-and-back trail near Pasadena. It is one of many trails located in Eaton Canyon Natural Area Park. The trail is classified as relatively easy to hike. Along the way, hikers will see a 40-foot waterfall and a small pool with views of the San Gabriel and Santa Monica mountains.

The trail is kid friendly, and dogs are also allowed as long as they are on a leash. With nice weather, the trailhead can get crowded on the weekends. When visiting, know that the trail might be closed during heavy rain. Wear comfortable and appropriate shoes, a hat, sunscreen, and thick socks. Make sure to carry extra water and a snack if needed.

The Eaton Canyon Natural Area Park offers equestrian trials, birdwatching, nature walks, and many other amenities beyond hiking.

Best Time to Visit: The Eaton Canyon Trail is open to the public Wednesday through Sunday from 8:00 a.m. to 5:00 p.m.

Pass/Permit/Fees: The Eaton Canyon Trail is free to enjoy. Free on-site parking is also available. Guests are asked to refrain from parking on the street.

Physical Address:
Eaton Canyon Trail Head
1999 Veranada Avenue
Pasadena, CA 91107

GPS Coordinates: 34.17913° N, 118.09658° W

Did You Know? Los Angeles County has nearly 60 hiking trails to enjoy.

Mount Wilson Observatory

The Mount Wilson Observatory was founded in 1904. Shortly after it was founded, studies at the observatory led it to become the world's foremost astronomical research facility. Today, the 100-inch telescope that helped researchers understand new theories about astronomy is still in use.

Visitors can view the Hooker 100-inch telescope that made history for free. To see the rest of the facility and other telescopes or learn more about the history of the observatory, tickets can be purchased for a two-hour tour. The Astronomical Museum located on the property is free of charge. The Mount Wilson Observatory also allows self-guided tours.

For those with respiratory conditions, limited mobility, or heart issues, the high elevation of the observatory might cause complications. It should also be noted that the observatory is not ADA compliant except for the Astronomical Museum and the Cosmic Café.

Best Time to Visit: The Mount Wilson Observatory is open Monday through Saturday from 10:00 a.m. to 5:00 p.m. The Cosmic Café is only open April through November on weekends from 9:00 a.m. to 5:00 p.m.

Pass/Permit/Fees: A daily parking pass can be purchased at the Cosmic Café or several other LA locations for $5.

Physical Address:
Mount Wilson Observatory
Mount Wilson
Sierra Madre, CA 91024

GPS Coordinates: 34.22542° N, 118.05729° W

Did You Know? Since space has no atmosphere, sound cannot travel there, meaning space is entirely silent.

Glen Ivy Hot Springs

Glen Ivy Hot Springs is the perfect place to stop, rejuvenate, and reset. The mineral spring pools and peaceful landscaping provide complete serenity, but a visit to Glen Ivy Hot Springs does require some planning. First, any group reservations should be under 12 people. Second, the minimum age is 18. Official forms of identification and cell phone numbers are required. Visitors are also encouraged to bring a refillable, non-glass tumbler. The tumblers should be empty when entering the facility.

Please note that Glen Ivy Hot Springs does not accept cash. Any charges while in the facility will be placed on the card on file. Consider wearing an old or dark swimsuit if booking time in Club Mud. Additionally, flip-flops, sandals, sunscreen, and a hat are recommended. Towels are provided, and robes can be rented for $20.

Best Time to Visit: Glen Ivy Hot Springs are open every day from 9:30 a.m. to 5:00 p.m. For appointments first thing in the morning, guests are allowed entry at 9:00 am.

Pass/Permit/Fees: Fees differ depending on the services selected. Parking is free.

Physical Address:
Glen Ivy Hot Springs
25000 Glen Ivy Road
Corona, CA 92883

GPS Coordinates: 33.75669° N, 117.49393° W

Did You Know? With over 300 hot springs, Nevada has more than any other state.

Van Buren Drive-In Theatre
and Swap Meet

The Van Buren Drive-In Theatre and Swap Meet is a fun place to visit that offers movies every day of the week. The swap meet is open Tuesday through Thursday and on the weekend. Visitors to the drive-in can enjoy first-run movies on the big screen from their vehicles. The price of admission includes two movies for the price of one unless the movie is single billed.

Audio for the movies is through an FM transmitter, which means it will run through the car radio. Concessions are offered on site or you can bring your own. The swap meet has over 300 vendors and runs from 6:00 a.m. to 2:00 p.m.

Best Time to Visit: The drive-in theater is open seven nights a week. Check the website for showtimes. The swap meet is open from 6:00 a.m. to 2:00 p.m. every day but Monday and Friday.

Pass/Permit/Fees: Parking is free. Drive-in prices are $10 for adults and $1 for children ages 5 to 9. Admission for the swap meet is free on Tuesday and Wednesday, $0.50 on Thursday, and $0.75 on the weekend.

Physical Address:
Van Buren Drive-In Theatre and Swap Meet
3035 Van Buren Boulevard
Riverside, CA 92503

GPS Coordinates: 34176° N, 117.44206° W

Did You Know? The Shankweiler's Drive-In Theatre in Orefield, PA, is the oldest drive-in theater in the United States.

Baldwin Hills Scenic Overlook

Baldwin Hills Scenic Overlook provides a fantastic view of Los Angeles. The view extends from the Los Angeles Basin to Santa Monica Bay, then towards the San Gabriel Mountains. Baldwin Hills Scenic Overlook is a 57-acre park that's also home to a visitor center and botanical gardens.

Access to the Baldwin Hills Scenic Overlook is available by stairs or by hiking a dirt loop trail that is a mile and a quarter in length. The trail zigzags back and forth, often crossing the stairs in case you start hiking and decide it's too much. The trail and stairs are family friendly, but be mindful that there is no shade, and no dogs are allowed. Be sure to dress appropriately, wear sunscreen, and bring water. It takes an average of 43 minutes to hike the trail.

The view will be worth it once you reach the top. Visitors often enjoy pointing out the Getty Center, the famous Hollywood sign, Griffith Observatory, and more. It's the perfect opportunity for a picture that encapsulates all LA has to offer.

Best Time to Visit: The overlook is open from 6:00 a.m. to 9:00 p.m. seven days a week.

Pass/Permit/Fees: Parking is available along the south side of Jefferson Boulevard at the base of the park or at the visitor center for $6.

Physical Address:
Baldwin Hills Scenic Overlook
6300 Hetzler Road
Culver City, CA 90232

GPS Coordinates: 34.15840° N, 118.38190° W

Did You Know? There are 282 stairs to the top of Baldwin Hills Scenic Overlook.

Smorgasburg LA

Smorgasburg LA is the largest open-air food market in the country. It operates in five other locations besides LA. With nearly 100 vendors on site, visitors have the chance to sample a variety of food from different cultures. There is a cinnamon bun specialist as well as high-end boba.

An up-to-date list of vendors is online. Be mindful that this list may change.

In addition to food vendors, you can shop at small businesses for everything from jewelry to clothing to home décor. The market is open rain or shine, so be sure to bring an umbrella. However, in the event of rain, not all vendors will open. Pets are not allowed.

Best Time to Visit: Smorgasburg LA is open every Sunday from 10:00 a.m. to 4:00 p.m.

Pass/Permit/Fees: The event is free to attend. There is no age limit, but ID is required to enter the beer garden. Parking is available on site.

Physical Address:
Smorgasburg LA
777 S. Alameda Street
Los Angeles, CA 90021

GPS Coordinates: 34.0351° N, 118.2417° W

Did You Know? Many people think that bubble tea is named for the boba tapioca balls, but it actually refers to the bubbly foam on top of the drink when shaken.

Walt Disney Concert Hall

The Walt Disney Concert Hall is one of four concert halls at the Los Angeles Music Center. It's hard to miss the wavy design of the building that opened in 2003. Designed by architect Frank Gehry, more than 6,000 curved panels look like waves of music floating through the air.

The Walt Disney Concert Hall is home to the LA Philharmonic and the Los Angeles Master Chorale. It's a state-of-the-art concert hall that's considered one of the most acoustically sophisticated in the world. The auditorium has 2,265 seats, and thanks to the technology incorporated, every seat offers prime listening.

The Walt Disney Concert Hall does not allow food or drink in the auditorium, but there are dining options available in the main lobby.

Best Time to Visit: The Walt Disney Concert Hall has a calendar of events posted online. Be sure to look for free events while in LA.

Pass/Permit/Fees: Parking for the Walt Disney Concert Hall is located on 2nd Street between Hope Street and Grand Avenue. The daily rate is $10 for events. Tickets for concerts at the Walt Disney Concert Hall vary depending on selection.

Physical Address:
Walt Disney Concert Hall
111 S. Grand Avenue
Los Angeles, CA 90012

GPS Coordinates: 34.0553° N, 118.2498° W

Did You Know? There are 44 instruments in a full orchestra. The string family of instruments makes up over half the total number.

Korean Bell of Friendship

The Korean Bell of Friendship can be found in the San Pedro neighborhood of Los Angeles. The bell was a gift from the South Korean government to the United States to demonstrate the friendship between the two countries.

The Korean Bell of Friendship is struck on the first Saturday of every month at noon. Additionally, it has also been struck on New Year's Eve, the Fourth of July, and Korean American Day on January 13th.

The Korean Bell of Friendship has been seen in multiple movies and television shows, including *The Usual Suspects*. The bell itself is a cast bronze bell that's mounted on a wood and stone pavilion. The bell is 12 feet high.

When visiting the bell, guests are encouraged to stay and enjoy the scenery. It is said that the area around the bell is perfect for kite flying thanks to the winds from the nearby ocean.

Best Time to Visit: The Korean Bell of Friendship can be seen 7 days a week between 7:00 a.m. and 7:00 p.m.

Pass/Permit/Fees: The Korean Bell is considered public art and is free to enjoy. Free parking is available on site.

Physical Address:
Korean Bell of Friendship
3601 S. Gaffey Street
San Pedro, CA 90731

GPS Coordinates: 33.7097° N, 118.2938° W

Did You Know? The Liberty Bell at Independence Hall is the most well-known bell in the United States. It was first made in 1972.

Rose Bowl Flea Market

The Rose Bowl Flea Market has been open for more than 50 years, offering a unique shopping experience for visitors. It is considered to be one of the most well-attended flea markets in the country, with hundreds of vendors and even more treasures.

Visitors can download a map of the Rose Bowl Flea Market, which is color coded by section. VIP admission is available, offering early admission for shoppers who want to start their day off with bargain hunting.

Shoppers should wear comfortable shoes and be mindful of the weather. The Rose Bowl Flea Market is open rain or shine. Food and beverages are available on site, offering everything from hot dogs to sushi.

Best Time to Visit: The Rose Bowl Flea Market is open to the general public at 9:00 a.m. on the second Sunday of every month. VIP entry begins at 5:00 am. The market closes at 4:00 p.m.

Pass/Permit/Fees: Parking for the market is free. Regular admission is $12 per person. VIP Admission is $20 per person. Tickets must be purchased online.

Physical Address:
Rose Bowl Flea Market (Rose Bowl Stadium)
1001 Rose Bowl Drive
Pasadena, CA 91103

GPS Coordinates: 34.1613° N, 118.1676° W

Did You Know? The Brimfield Flea Market in Hampden County, MA, is the nation's oldest flea market.

116

Raging Waters Water Park

Raging Waters Water Park is the perfect place to spend a warm summer day. With over 23 acres of fun, Raging Waters is the largest water park in Los Angeles. In addition to the 350,000-gallon wave pool, guests can enjoy a 60-foot water slide with twists and turns at every corner, an enclosed water shoot that is 200 feet in the air, Pirate's Cove splash park, and more. On sunny days, you can take cover under rented cabanas or bring your own pop-up beach shelters. Shelters should be no more than 8 x 5 feet. Please note that stakes cannot be put in the ground, so bring weights as well. For safety, complimentary life jackets are available. They are required for guests under 48 inches tall regardless of swimming ability.

Outside food and beverages are not allowed in the water park. There are dining options available, offering everything from hamburgers to salads to fruit. If you need storage while at Raging Waters Water Park, keyless electronic lockers are available.

Best Time to Visit: Raging Waters Water Park opens for the season in late May. Check the calendar online for operating hours or to purchase tickets.

Pass/Permit/Fees: Parking permits are available from the parking booth attendant or at self-serve pay stations. Parking is $6 per car during the week and $10 per car on weekends or holidays. Tickets for the park start at $54.99.

Physical Address:
Raging Waters Water Park
111 Raging Waters Drive
San Dimas, CA 91773

GPS Coordinates: 34° 5' 28.4208'' N, 117° 48' 44.5068'' W

Did You Know? At 70 acres, Noah's Park in the Wisconsin Dells is the nation's largest water park.

Proper Planning

With this guide, you are well on your way to properly planning a marvelous adventure. When you plan your travels, you should become familiar with the area, save any maps to your phone for access without internet, and bring plenty of water—especially during the summer months. Depending on which adventure you choose, you will also want to bring snacks or even a lunch. For younger children, you should do your research and find destinations that best suit your family's needs. You should also plan when and where to get gas, local lodgings, and food. We've done our best to group these destinations based on nearby towns and cities to help make planning easier.

Dangerous Wildlife

There are several dangerous animals and insects you may encounter while hiking. With a good dose of caution and awareness, you can explore safely. Here are steps you can take to keep yourself and your loved ones safe from dangerous flora and fauna while exploring:

- Keep to the established trails.
- Do not look under rocks, leaves, or sticks.
- Keep hands and feet out of small crawl spaces, bushes, covered areas, or crevices.
- Wear long sleeves and pants to keep arms and legs protected.
- Keep your distance should you encounter any dangerous wildlife or plants.

Limited Cell Service

Do not rely on cell service for navigation or emergencies. Always have a map with you and let someone know where you are and how long you intend to be gone, just in case.

First Aid Information

Always travel with a first aid kit in case of emergencies.

Here are items you should be certain to include in your primary first aid kit:

- Nitrile gloves
- Blister care products
- Band-Aids in multiple sizes and waterproof type
- Ace wrap and athletic tape
- Alcohol wipes and antibiotic ointment
- Irrigation syringe
- Tweezers, nail clippers, trauma shears, safety pins
- Small zip-lock bags containing contaminated trash

It is recommended to also keep a secondary first aid kit, especially when hiking, for more serious injuries or medical emergencies. Items in this should include:

- Blood clotting sponges
- Sterile gauze pads
- Trauma pads
- Second-skin/burn treatment
- Triangular bandages/sling
- Butterfly strips
- Tincture of benzoin
- Medications (ibuprofen, acetaminophen, antihistamine, aspirin, etc.)
- Thermometer

- CPR mask
- Wilderness medicine handbook
- Antivenin

There is much more to explore, but this is a great start.

For information on all national parks, visit https://www.nps.gov/index.htm .

This site will give you information on up-to-date entrance fees and how to purchase a park pass for unlimited access to national and state parks. This site will also introduce you to all of the trails at each park.

Always check before you travel to destinations to make sure there are no closures. Some hiking trails close when there is heavy rain or snow in the area and other parks close parts of their land for the migration of wildlife. Attractions may change their hours or temporarily shut down for various reasons. Check the websites for the most up-to-date information.

www.ingramcontent.com/pod-product-compliance
Lightning Source LLC
LaVergne TN
LVHW021514080426
835509LV00018B/2511